The Supervisor Handbook: What They Don't Teach You About Leadership

Joshua Hagen

Table of Contents

Acknowledgements

This book would not be possible without the fantastic mentors and leaders that I have been blessed to work with and observe over the years. Thanks to Phil Batton, Jared Burdick, Nathan Burdick, Richard Colvin, Sarah Schaefer, Ron Williams, Denny Bray, Sherry Patti, Katie Welch and all the phenomenal supervisors that I have been blessed to have worked with over the years! Special thank you to Audrea Hagen and Marten Roos. Most importantly, I would like to thank my wife Erin Hagen for recognizing my vision and being supportive of the long hours and time spent creating successful teams.

Introduction

When I started writing this book, I was approaching it strictly from a sales perspective. I love sales! I loved it when I was on the frontlines as a sales professional! However, what I love even more is helping people succeed! A couple of chapters in, I realized that what I was writing not only applies to leading in a sales environment, but really encompasses aspects of being a leader in any setting. While I truly believe that everything we do in life comes back to sales in some form, I recognized that there would be a greater impact and value for anyone wanting to become a great leader if this book wasn't just focused on sales leadership. I hope as you read this book you'll recognize some of the ways that sales and leadership go hand in hand. Matter of fact, in some cases, I'll blatantly point them out. This is designed to help people in all walks of life and in all positions within the workforce have greater, more satisfying relationships with their leaders and co-workers by being able to utilize some of the communication techniques I have learned over the years in sales. A large part of anyone's success is influenced by the people around them and that includes their manager or leader. Good leaders have the ability to influence and guide those that report to them to greater success than those employees may have ever dreamed possible. Bad managers can discourage and demotivate a good employee before they're even able to really get started! I am writing this book for current leaders or aspiring leaders that want to help their teams and organizations have not only success, but job satisfaction and a fantastic relationship with their leader as well.

My Journey into Leadership

My name is Joshua Hagen and I am the founder of Shining Beacon Leadership. I created Shining Beacon Leadership to help grow and develop leaders. This may be the young employee who wants to grow into a leadership position, or it may be for the seasoned leader who is looking to expand their skills and become an even better leader for their team or their company. I believe that we have a severe leadership problem in today's society that could easily be solved by more investment in developing the skills and communication habits that leaders need to be successful. By doing this we will be creating a world where employees feel better about the companies they work for, the leaders they work with, and what they do for a living. The welcomed consequence will be greater results for companies because they'll have inspired and engaged employees and leaders.

I am passionate about leadership development for multiple reasons. I want to share my story with you so that you can see how my past has helped ignite that passion for developing leaders. Some people say that leaders are born and not made. I actually feel the opposite. I believe that leaders are made and not born. I myself am one of those cases. Growing up I was a fairly shy and introverted person. I was never the type to want attention or be in the spotlight. I did have a strong sense of what I felt was right and wrong and I tended to let that guide the person I was to become. Maybe that was my early leadership quality? I don't know. However, it's not something I was very vocal about. If I saw someone hurting, either mentally or physically, I would try and comfort them and do what I could to help improve their situation, but it wasn't something that I was going to draw a lot of attention to. Even today, I lean towards being the person that leads by example rather than being the most outgoing or vocal despite my twenty plus years in sales and leadership!

I began working at twelve years old when I started delivering newspapers in Vancouver, Washington for the local newspaper. This is where I got my first taste of having a "boss" and very quickly realized that some were better than others. When I turned sixteen I got a job at a local natural foods grocery store and experienced the same thing. I found that some of the managers there were definitely better than others. At that age I wasn't really thinking much about it but looking back I can now see some of the qualities that made "good" leaders and some of the qualities that made "bad" leaders. At eighteen I went back to working for the local newspaper, but this time I was the one managing the young newspaper carriers. While I didn't really consider that to be a leadership position at the time, I still always made the effort to set the best possible example for the carriers I was managing, most of whom were twelve to fourteen-year old boys. At twenty years old I got my first real sales job selling fitness equipment in a call center. It was there that I learned how important it is to learn something from every leader you have. While most of my direct supervisors were fine, there were some in the company that I observed and vowed to never be like. At that point in my life I had no aspirations to be a leader or manage people, but it was clear to me that if I was ever in that position there were things I would avoid doing like the plague! It ended up being one of the best lessons I could have learned because it stayed with me all the way until I was running a call center. Every day I wanted to make sure I was not creating an environment like the one I observed at that first call center. After leaving that company I worked for a short period of time as a collector and then for a company selling a real estate lead management system in Bellevue, Washington. Another important lesson I learned while working there is that just because someone was a top performer in their current position, it doesn't necessarily mean that it will translate into them being a great leader.

After moving back to Beaverton, Oregon from Bellevue, Washington I began working for a company selling wireless phones. This is where I feel like I got to experience truly excellent leadership. It all started with my District Manager. What stood out to me immediately is how he would take the time to check-in with each employee to see how they were doing, would actively coach to help with skill improvement and would have the tough conversations when necessary. I recall going through a tough time with a health issue that forced me to leave work unexpectedly on multiple occasions. The District Manager met with me one on one and asked what I was going through. He genuinely cared and ended up giving me some advice that helped me persevere through that tough and even scary time in my life. The conversation and support I felt stayed with me to the point where I've now had very similar conversations with employees that have reported to me! In many cases it has helped them through their tough times as well. I am forever grateful to that manager for having the courage to talk with me about my situation and then share with me what I could do from his point of view to help me through it. Managers that don't care don't take the time to have those types of conversations.

It just so happened that I ended up reporting directly to the District Manager's brother at a new store I was moved to. It was there that I learned the value of truly leading by example. The store manager would never ask us as the employees to do something that he wouldn't do himself. While he was a very demanding leader, it was evident that he was putting in even more work than we were and wouldn't sit back on his position as the store manager to get out of some of the more tedious tasks of the store. One thing that stood out to me the most about this leader was that even with all the additional responsibilities he had on his plate he still put himself on the schedule to clean the store bathroom. This is easily something he could have delegated to the other employees in the store, but he chose to be in the trenches with us in every aspect. He took a true interest in his employees, created a great yet competitive environment and was always looking for opportunities to help us improve.

At this point in my life I had zero desire to move into a leadership position. I loved selling and enjoyed the fact that I didn't have to put in what seemed like sixty plus hours a week like the previously mentioned leaders. I had moved on to a different company and was seeing success as a sales professional. It's here that I learned how powerful even some simple encouragement can be. I had an assistant manager who asked me if I had ever thought about moving into leadership. She said she saw the way I interacted with the rest of the team and my contributions during team meetings and told me that I should consider a role in leadership. That was the spark I needed! From then on, while still focusing on my individual sales, I made it my mission to have the people that sat at the desks around me be the best performers on our team of fourteen. I wanted to be able to have my boss put people near me and know that he would see an increase in their sales. Any time I wasn't on a call I focused on motivating the people around me and providing any tips to help them improve their results.

While I didn't get the first promotion opportunity after shifting my focus to becoming a leader in the organization, I took the feedback and continued to develop my leadership qualities and speaking abilities. About six months later another assistant manager position became available and this time I was ready! Ever since then, I've continued to educate myself on how to lead, motivate and communicate. I took all the lessons I learned as a young sales professional, both positive and negative, to help guide how I would lead my teams. I vowed never to lead like some I had witnessed and always attempt to lead like the best leaders I had observed. I watched and spent a lot of time learning from my peers and analyzing things that my bosses and even their bosses did that I liked and some that I disliked to help me become the best possible leader that I could. I continue to regularly ask for feedback and do a lot of self-reflection to help me with my opportunities or blind-spots and then work to make improvements. I know I'm not perfect by any means and am always looking for ways to better myself.

This has been my journey into leadership. I don't consider myself to be a natural leader. This story is the reason that I say I feel leaders are made and not born. I hope you'll join me on this journey as we make the world a better place through stronger leadership! It takes a strong desire in the person that eventually does end up being a leader to want to learn, grow, do what's best and right and truly cares about people. I don't think you'll ever see a great leader who doesn't truly care about people. Looking back, I did exhibit some leadership qualities while growing up, but for the most part I was generally introverted and shy. Even during my first couple of years while in formal leadership positions, whenever I had to get up and speak in front of a group my heart would start to pound, my palms would get sweaty and I would wonder "can I do this"? It took repeated practice to get to a point where I felt confident eventually standing in front of hundreds of people and speaking on a topic. In writing this book, I will be drawing from over twenty years of personal sales and leadership experience. I will do my best to give you the good, the bad and the ugly of what I've witnessed over the years. Some of it will be designed to inspire you to action and some of it will be designed for you to know what to avoid like the plague! I will use real life examples to illustrate how small choices can make a big impact on the people you lead. I am confident that if you read this book with an open mind and willingness to try new things, you will gain new strategies to help lead your team to new heights. It is my hope that you will be both educated and entertained. Let's get into it...

Chapter One: Gaining Buy-In & Establishing Credibility

Probably the most important thing you can do when leading a team of any sort is to get the buy-in from those that you are leading and establish your credibility. Without this, you will not be able to maximize results, nor truly help people reach their full potential. Your team needs to know that you are there for them and that your goal is to help them become as successful as possible as fast as possible.

How do you establish credibility? It certainly helps if you've performed the work or been in the role that you are now leading. However, this isn't something that will make or break you when it comes to leading your new team. It just means that you will need to establish credibility in other ways to gain the trust of your team. I recommend doing this by having the courage to show some vulnerability and ask questions of the team to learn specifics of the position and how it relates to them.

A method that I've found to be successful is to jump in and actually do the work alongside your employees. You're not expected to be amazing since you don't do that job regularly. Your team will see your willingness to get in the trenches with them, gaining firsthand experience, and you will be rewarded with the buy-in and respect of your team. This is going to help when you're coaching for improvement as you can speak from experience and not just numbers on a spreadsheet.

Any time there is a change in leadership there is going to be fear and excitement. People are going to be wondering; "is this leader going to clean house?" "Is my job at risk?" "Why was this person chosen?" "Are they going to be a micromanager?" One of your first priorities should be to get the entire team together for a team meeting. The goal of this meeting is primarily to let them get to know you. Who are you? What is your background? What brought you to the company, or to this team in particular? What is your leadership philosophy? This meeting will most likely alleviate fears and anxiety in some and increase it in others. That's OK! We all have been on teams where there are people who do a fantastic job and are great teammates and others who should have left the business long ago either because of poor performance or a poor attitude. When the meeting is over, the ones that do a great job should be excited about the prospect of working with you and the ones that don't do such a great job should be thinking about how they are going to improve or decide to move on from the business.

After the initial team meeting, the next priority should be to meet with the individuals on your team. This is where you are going to be able to spend time getting to know them. The best leaders I have observed have been able to learn about the individuals on their team and are then able to relate something that interests that individual back to the new leader. In this way, you are continuing to build your credibility while creating an emotional connection with the individuals on your team. Studies have shown that people connect with other people who are like them. This gives you an opportunity to get to know your team on an individual level and build that connection. This will also come in handy when you are coaching for improvement, as you will be able to relate the situation to something meaningful to them. Make a connection with them and my experience has been that the probability of success increases.

During this meeting you will also begin the discussion on what their goals and aspirations are. Spend time asking questions about where they see themselves in a year. What will they have accomplished? What will they have done inside and outside of work? How can you, as the leader, help them achieve what they want to achieve whether it be at work or outside of it? I have found that you will always get better performance if you provide the WIIFM-what's in it for me- and relate how improved performance will help the employee get what they want.

After you have held these meetings and began to establish their trust in you as the leader, it is important to hold a follow up meeting. During this meeting the goal is to get the team talking about what they liked and disliked about previous leadership. This is not a gripe session where you are asking them to bad-mouth their previous leader. Should it go that way, you have the responsibility to bring the meeting back to its purpose. This should be a solution focused meeting with the desired outcome being a greater working relationship for all parties involved. Think of it as a start/stop/continue type of session. You are going to learn what worked well, what they would like you to continue doing, as well as what may have previously caused friction, burnout and poor performance. Make sure that it is framed in a way that will guide you on how to work best with the team. Don't let the message be muddled into them thinking that you are going to implement or do everything that you learn. I have seen instances where poor performing teams want a new leader to continue with some of the past practices that led to the removal of the previous leader. Obviously, that's not going to work well for anyone...especially you as the new leader in the role!

One exercise that I have both observed and done myself, is to ask the team "what makes a perfect leader?" On a sheet of paper, write down everything that they feel makes a perfect leader. Feel free to have further discussion if something is unclear or that not everyone in the group agrees on. Using a different sheet of paper take down the answers to the question "what makes a bad leader?" Finally, on a third sheet of paper record the answers to "what do we want to be known for?" I have found that in most cases, what the team wants and what the leader wants are going to be very similar or at least work in synergy with each other. You will always be more effective if you have gotten the team to participate and verbalize what it is that they want to be known for as everyone is then accountable to it.

There is one, very important part to all of this that I haven't mentioned yet. I imagine that some of you have been reading this and thinking "this sounds like manipulation." Without one integral piece I might agree with you. Here's what it is-you truly do have to care about the individuals on your team and be willing to do what's necessary to help them achieve their goals. If you don't truly care about helping your team members achieve their goals, you are most likely just manipulating them for your own gain. The ideas I've written about in this chapter are an extremely powerful step for your team to gain trust in you, buy-in to your message and establish your credibility. You cannot take that power lightly or for granted. Being ingenuine when using this method will cause you to be seen as a phony who only cares about the bottom line. Use this method with a genuine care and respect for your employees and you may be recognized as the best leader they have ever had the pleasure of working with.

Do What's in The Best Interest of Your Employees

If you just look at that statement "do what's in the best interest of your employees" you may think, isn't that being too soft? I think the opposite is true. Sometimes doing what's in your employee's best interest is actually very difficult for both parties. However, this should always be one of your guiding principles. If you're looking to do what's best for them, regardless of it being difficult or not, they will recognize that fact and respect you for it.

Let's dive into this a little bit deeper. Every one of your people is going to have their own individual strengths and weaknesses. You would be doing everyone, including yourself, a disservice by taking a "one size fits all" approach. The "one size fits all" approach will not work, and you won't establish any credibility as the leader. Instead, identify what areas can help the individual maximize their performance. I recall having an employee who had a phenomenal sales closing percentage. She was one of the best in our organization…however, she wasn't making the kind of money that she wanted to make or that I knew she was capable of. The reason was that there were times where she was spending too much time with the customer prior to wrapping up the sale as well as her being slower with the order entry system. I could have done what previous supervisors had done with her and simply praised her for having one of the highest closing percentages in the organization. I couldn't do that! I knew that she had certain goals and income aspirations because of our one on one conversation about her goals and what she wanted to accomplish inside of and outside of work. If I had

17

taken the approach of just praising her out of fear that any constructive criticism might upset her and cause a temporary decrease in performance (therefore affecting my overall team numbers since she was the top in closing percentage) she would stay at the level she was at. When a person gets stagnant they tend to look for something else that will allow them to earn more income and will help them achieve her goals. As this was a fantastic employee I absolutely did not want to lose her! Here's what I did…I sat down with the employee and praised her excellent results in terms of her closing percentage. We then recapped what her personal goals were and what kind of income she wanted to earn. This got her thinking about what she wanted, not what I wanted, and put her in a receptive mood for feedback. We then discussed how what she was doing was getting her good results, but they weren't getting her the kind of results that would help her achieve what she ultimately wanted to accomplish. Together we came up with a plan to help her streamline her questions in the sales process to make it a more efficient call while still gathering all of the necessary information. More importantly, we came up with a way for her to eliminate distractions that caused her to be less efficient while working in the order entry system. The end result was that she consistently increased her paychecks by implementing what we had discussed and within six months was able to accomplish her goal of buying her own home. Some managers would have left well enough alone since she was performing well. I knew that she could accomplish more and by doing what was in the best interest of the employee I was able to help her achieve her goals much faster and at the same time retain an excellent employee. I cared about her and her goals and had the courage to risk upsetting a top performer because ultimately, it was in her best interest.

This can also go another way. Sometimes doing what's in the best interest of the employee means letting them go to find other opportunities for employment. As leaders, oftentimes we feel bad when having to terminate someone's employment and let them go. That's natural. Very few people like the feeling of having to let someone go. It's a major impact on their, and their families lives. I've found that as difficult as it is to have to let someone go, many times it is actually in their best interest. Think about a time where you were in a job or position that you either hated or weren't successful in. More often than not the two tend to go hand in hand. You may not have believed in the product or maybe it was the processes with which you had to do your work. You toiled away, day after day, miserable in what you were doing. Humans are creatures of habit and in most cases also don't like change. It shouldn't be a surprise that, after the initial shock, many are relieved that they are free to find employment elsewhere and have the opportunity to do something that they actually enjoy doing.

Here's a real-life example that I experienced. We had a long-time employee where it was evident that they had simply burned out. Despite his direct supervisor and my best attempts to break them out of the funk, they could (or would) not pull themselves out of it. Eventually, it came to a point where we had to terminate his employment. This was especially difficult because this particular employee was friends with one of my friends outside of work. The truth was that the termination needed to happen as the employee was not achieving the results needed of him even after coaching had been provided. I looked at this as a case where termination was doing what was best for the employee based on the obvious burn out and despite the attempts to get them reengaged. This opinion was validated about a year later when I saw the former employee at an event that our mutual friend was hosting. The former employee came up to me and let me know that there were no hard feelings and that being let go was one of the best things that could have happened to him. He stated that while it was true that he was making less money overall in his new job, he was much happier with life in general and felt a better sense of accomplishment. He was even physically and mentally healthier while working in his new role with his new company. I thanked him for sharing that with me and we raised a glass to new opportunities.

Whenever I've had an employee that I've had to let go, if I know someone that they're friends with, I'll still follow up on how the former employee is doing. In most cases, I'll hear that they're doing wonderfully and ended up landing on their feet with a great new opportunity that fits them better. Therefore, I can confidently say that sometimes doing what's in the best interest of the employee actually does mean letting them go to find other opportunities.

One of the most impactful things you can do as a leader is to build credibility with your team early on. This can be done many different ways. I've found that taking time as a group to learn what's important to the team overall as well as taking time with individuals to learn their personal strengths and opportunities are both very important. It does take time, but it will be one of the best investments you can make in your team and your future success in leading that team. In addition, trying to always look through the lens of doing what's in the best interest of your employees is another way that you'll build credibility. The fact that you care enough to try and see things from their perspective and let that help guide the decisions that are made will resonate and make a huge long-term impact.

Chapter Two: Learning Your Team

There are two different approaches you're going to take when learning your team. One approach will be to learn the group and the group dynamic and the other will be to sit down with each person on the team and get to know them individually. Both are extremely important. Let's jump into each strategy.

Getting to Know the Team

Set up a team meeting to get everyone together. This gives you an opportunity to learn the team dynamic. You'll observe how people behave in the meeting, their comfort levels with speaking up, how they treat their co-workers and even body language that can be an indicator of how they feel about others on the team, you or the company itself. Another very important piece of this meeting is for you to learn who the team leaders are. Each team has people that they look up to. Sometimes these people will be vocal in meetings and can either help or hurt the message you're trying to convey. It's important to know who those leaders are and be aware of how they are either going to further your vision or sabotage what you're trying to do with the team. Every leader needs a "player coach" and this is one of the quickest and easiest ways for you as a new team leader to determine who that person or those people will be for you. Refer to chapter one for some additional ideas of what to do during that first meeting.

Another powerful way to learn your new team and establish your credibility is to organize an off-site gathering. This can be something as simple as a meal out with the team that you pay for or something larger like an actual event. If the company budget won't permit it, don't be afraid to use your own money on this. I truly feel this is an extremely important component to building your team and bringing it together. Sometimes, if the team knows you are paying for the event out of your own pocket it builds even more credibility because it shows you are willing to sacrifice your own money for the good of the team. A team outing is a chance to informally learn more about your team. You're able to see how they are outside of work since just about everybody will be a little more relaxed outside of the office setting. This can go a long way, once again, in seeing how everyone interacts with and gets along with each other. Here are a few examples of things I've done to build team camaraderie and get to know the team better. With larger teams of up to fourteen people I would buy a birthday cake when someone on the team had a birthday and share it with the team during a team meeting. With smaller teams I would take the team out to lunch to a reasonably priced restaurant when someone had a birthday. This is something you can start right away by simply finding out when each person's birthday is. If there aren't any birthdays in the month you start, you can find out who had the most recent birthday and do a "late" birthday celebration to start things off.

Other ideas I've either done myself or seen done include outings to places like Top Golf, laser tag, bowling, renting a movie theater for a team movie, a team cooking class, trips to a mountain for a day of playing in the snow, beach trips, sporting events and for those who are a little more daring…skydiving. Although, I don't recommend skydiving unless you've

23

got the go ahead from everyone on the team. Again, in some cases the budget has been provided by the company and in others the leader has paid out of pocket knowing that the investment in the team would pay back greatly!

Getting to Know the Individual

Just as important as getting to know the team, if not more important, is getting to know the individuals on your team. I recall a time when a leader of mine, that I had directly or indirectly reported to for almost nine years and had considered a mentor and fantastic leader, was abruptly let go from the company. I was devastated and even considered leaving the company at that time. When the new leader was hired one of the first things he did was take the time to sit down with everyone and learn about them. My first meeting with him had very little to do with business and was almost entirely about who I was outside of work. We connected over a common love for, of all things, professional wrestling. Subsequent meetings had more to do with what my career aspirations were and how we could accomplish both of our goals with the company through working together. We ended up having a fantastic relationship with me learning a great deal from him until I left the company to pursue a career advancement opportunity with a new company in a different state. Something I learned later was that he was told that I would be the most difficult to connect with of his new direct reports due to my relationship and admiration of the previous leader. I imagine that he did this for all his new direct reports, but I found out that he had done some research on who I was and what I liked outside of work prior to our first meeting. He already had it in his head that he would use our common interest of professional wrestling as a way "in". We've all heard the saying that "people buy from people they like" and to me this was a genius way of gaining buy-in. Even though neither of us are with that same company any longer we still keep in touch.

Some of the things you'll want to make sure and cover during your first couple of one on one meetings include: what is their background, how long have they been in their role, what are their career aspirations, what help would they like in achieving their goals with the company or otherwise, what are their major strengths and what do they see as their major areas of opportunity. Some other things that are important to learn about your direct reports are things like what is their learning style, how do they like to be managed, what are some attributes of the best leader they ever worked for and on the other hand what were some of the attributes of the worst boss they ever had. Learning these things about your new team members are going to give you insight into how they like to work and how they like to be managed. It can help you know what techniques to utilize in managing the individual as well as some things you may want to avoid in order to maximize the working relationship. I have found that this very simple act of recognizing the individuals learning style goes a long way in achieving the end results that you want to achieve. The reason for this is that you now know what resonates best with that individual and you can tailor your message to their unique abilities. I have had employees tell me that they learned more from me in just a few months than they had in years working under previous leaders. It wasn't because I was sharing any mind-blowing techniques or ideas with them…it all just came down to me presenting information to them in a way that they were best able to process it.

A very true, but unfortunate reality of getting to know your team is also knowing who needs to stay and who probably needs to go. I'm the type of person who likes to give everyone a chance and will trust until my trust has been betrayed. As you're learning your team, you will learn who fits your vision, team culture, and who's open to new ideas. You'll also learn who has maybe maxed out in their current role and needs to be moved into a different role or possibly out of the company altogether. Please don't take this as a "fire everyone that doesn't work like you" type of statement. As a matter of fact, I have found that by learning the individuals on your team you end up needing to fire less often. This is because you can speak directly to what will be meaningful to the employee and help them understand new concepts more quickly. However, if they are truly poor employees, especially in both performance and attitude, then they do need to be shown the door and provided an opportunity to seek employment elsewhere. If you have someone on the team who is good for the company, but may not be best in their current role, by truly knowing their strengths and opportunities you will oftentimes be able to help them get into a better position within the company that is beneficial for both the employee and the organization. I'm proud to say that I've been able to help numerous employees, who were good fits for the company but not good fits in their role, find different positions that maximized their skill sets and were mutually beneficial for all parties involved.

Getting to know your team is integral to being a great leader and should be prioritized as something you'll want to do as soon as possible. In doing so, you will achieve results faster than you may have even thought possible. Here's a breakdown of some of the benefits that you'll gain by prioritizing getting to know your team...

- You'll know who your "player coaches" are that you can lean on to help you with messaging.
- You'll know the learning styles of the individuals on your team and how you can best communicate with them to get the result you desire.
- You'll have shown a genuine interest in who you're working with which is always appreciated.
- You'll have given yourself an idea of who best fits your team and the vision you're trying to achieve.

All these things together will help flesh out the road map of what work you'll need to do with your team. It will let you know if you truly have the best group of people to join you on your journey to fantastic results, or if you'll need to bring in some new talent to help you get where you want to go.

Chapter Three: Leading by Example

Leading by example is perhaps the most important thing you can do as a leader. When I think back over my career and the leaders that I've looked up to, all of them have been excellent at leading by example. One of my favorite stories that I've shared many times is when I worked for a company selling wireless phones. The store manager led in virtually all aspects of the store…he was the top salesperson, he made sure things ran smoothly in the store, he put in longer hours than anyone else and he made sure we had a great time while we were at work. The thing that impressed me most though was his willingness to get in and do the "dirty work" that he could have just as easily passed on since he had so many other duties. For example, we had a schedule for who would clean the store bathroom. Not the most glamorous job in the store. Instead of putting that task on the other workers in the store and saying that he had more important duties to handle (which he actually did) he also put himself on the schedule to clean the bathroom. There were times when he had to ask one of us to take on his slot because he was working on more important things, but the simple fact that he was willing to do that work made us very open to take on his spot when he needed us to step up. Jared Burdick is the first person who supervised me that I think of as a true leader. Years later, when asked to be a keynote speaker on the topic of leadership at a Coach's Camp, I went back to the things I learned by observing Jared and shared how I tried to model myself after him when I was a new leader.

You will always gain more respect from your employees if they see you "in the trenches". When I was a supervisor in a call center sales environment one of my favorite methods of coaching was to live listen and actually jump in with tips for the sales professional to close the sale or get more out of the sale. I would always make it a point to show the employee how much more money they earned because I jumped in and helped them with the sale. It established me as an expert and showed that I did know what I was talking about. I was leading by example, by basically doing the work just like the members on my team. The team appreciated knowing that I wasn't just someone who had never done the job and was now telling them what to do. I could demonstrate how to do the work effectively and in a way that, in many cases, was better than what they were doing on their own. Once I became a manager, leading the supervisors, I encouraged them to take the same approach. There were some supervisors who had never taken this approach to coaching, that experienced some of the best results they had ever achieved with their teams by making the adjustment. It is a lot of work. Much more than just sitting behind a computer telling people what to do like some supervisors do, but the reward is definitely worth it.

One time in my career where I made a huge mistake and didn't do a good job of leading by example was when I transitioned into a new industry with a product and selling method that I wasn't experienced in. While I have always been successful in sales, this was something different that I had not been involved with before. My primary role was to lead all aspects of the sales organization and increase revenue. While we made some big strides and improved revenue overall during my time with the company, I know that we could have achieved results faster had I taken a step back, gone through training just like any new employee and taken a couple of weeks where I was on the phones myself. This would have established credibility in me early on as I would have been seen as someone who had actually done the job and I would have known 100% what I was talking about. As it stood, I was learning a lot about the job from people that maybe didn't have the company's best interests at heart and it set me and the company back. While I did get on the phones from time to time to help close deals (and usually had a better closing percentage than those doing the closing on a daily basis) I believe it was too little too late. I left the company a little under a year after starting, and ultimately while I think the end outcome would have been the same, I do think that we would have achieved better, and faster results together had I taken a different approach early on.

You can never go wrong with leading by example. Throughout the years I have tried to take the approach of leading by example whenever possible. The biggest lesson for me was what I observed with Jared. There was nothing that he would ask us to do that he wouldn't do himself. This approach has always stuck with me and it is one of those fundamentals that I will always practice. Even in the previous example where I didn't achieve what I wanted to, it wasn't because I was unwilling to do the job myself. It just came down to a matter of not prioritizing correctly. While I understand that not everyone is going to be able to put in long hours due to their family life or individual schedules, one thing that has been consistent during my career in leadership is this feedback…my teams have told me that they see how hard I work and the long hours that I've put in and they're inspired to work even harder. This is one of the greatest compliments I think any leader can receive because it shows that you are truly leading by example!

Chapter Four: Coaching

I worked with someone once who did the bulk of their coaching through e-mail in order to increase productivity. When one of their employees was about to be terminated for poor performance the employee was able to save their job by claiming that they had never been coached. There hadn't been documented one on one coaching sessions, so the employee was permitted by HR to stay on. The employee said they hadn't read the coaching e-mails because "if it was important, my supervisor would just meet with me about it". While I didn't necessarily agree with either side of things, the coaching just through e-mail or the excuse that the employee didn't read the coaching because they didn't think it was important, the employee ended up being terminated a few months later after documented meetings had taken place and performance still wasn't improving. How you coach, how often you coach, and documentation of the coaching are all important aspects of this component of a leader's job.

I personally feel that the mark of a truly great leader comes down to their coaching and how they are able to help others become great at what they do. If a culture of coaching is established from the top, it will take root and permeate the rest of the company culture. After all, we know that the culture of the company starts with the top person. If the person at the top constantly creates an environment of fear and rules with an iron fist, the approach will have a trickle-down effect. If the person at the top encourages an environment where mistakes are OK as long as they are learned from and, better yet, coaches and guides to help avoid mistakes whenever possible it will also take root throughout the rest of the business.

The leader who is a true coach will always achieve greater results than the leader who just "manages" and cracks the whip. While there are times that it is necessary to manage, if that is the only approach you take you will not promote loyalty or have anyone go the extra mile in your organization. The true coach inspires loyalty by, as John C. Maxwell states, "knowing the way, going the way and most importantly, showing the way"! You've got to be willing to get your hands dirty and demonstrate a job well done if you're going to create truly loyal followers. Even in the case where the leader may not have done the particular job as the frontline employee, having the knowledge of the job and being able to demonstrate proficiency will go a long way in the eyes of the people reporting to that leader. There are many ways to coach, but for this chapter I want to dig into a few methods that I've used and taught over the years to have successful, high performing teams.

One on One Meeting

One of my favorite methods of coaching is the tried and true one on one meeting. I know this is not a preferred method by many, which I don't understand. Maybe it has to do with the thought of losing productivity while in the meeting or maybe it is the leader's discomfort with that more intimate one on one setting. My belief is that the productivity lost during a one on one meeting is far made up for in future performance. This is based on clear expectations being set and setting up the environment where the employee feels supported and is regularly enhancing their skills in their position. In addition, I believe there is a great deal of loyalty built through the more intimate one on one meeting setting. It is during this time that you can get to know your employee better as a person and truly understand their motivations and what makes them tick. I can't state enough how important it has been to my success as a leader to really get to know my employees, what drives them and what the best way to coach them will be. Everybody is going to be different and it is during these one on one meetings that you're able to best determine and learn directly from them what style is going to produce the greatest results.

My one on one meetings generally followed a pretty similar format which I'll break down here. The beginning of my meeting started with a little bit of small talk. In many cases it had to do with something personal that I happened to know about the employee. Maybe it was inquiring about their family, a recent event they attended, something they did or even progress on something they were doing outside of work. I want to be clear that it wasn't just small talk for the sake of small talk either. I truly wanted to know about the employee. Plus, in terms of motivating someone, if you know about them and what they like to do outside of work it can help with getting top performance inside the workplace as well. If they asked about me I would share, but if they didn't I wouldn't waste time going into what I was doing outside of work. After all, this meeting is about them not about you.

In most meetings I would go into it having an agenda of something that I wanted to discuss. It may be performance related both with recognition and areas of opportunity, a discussion on something we were working on to develop their skills or it may have been a particular interaction that they had with a customer. Admittedly, there were times where I didn't have an agenda at all and the meeting was simply meant to touch base with the employee. In any case the meeting almost always started with the same question…"so what do you have that you want to discuss with me today?" The beautiful thing to me about that question is this, in many cases they would bring up in some form what I had on the agenda anyway. Think about this…when you're being coached are you going to be more receptive when talking about something you want to talk about or when it is someone else giving you feedback on something you weren't expecting? The environment was set up for success because I was allowing them to begin. I would say roughly ninety percent of the time I would be able to tie back what I had on my agenda to whatever they had on their mind. I would consider that a win-win scenario!

In the rare case that we had completely different topics in mind, I made sure to still cover their concerns first. When something is important to someone it typically is the only thing on their mind, or at minimum the main thing they are thinking about. I wanted to make sure that we had addressed their concern first, so they could be fully open to whatever issue I also needed to discuss with them. By ensuring they felt heard and satisfied that their issues were addressed, I felt that they were then more open to discussing other topics that also needed to be covered. Make sure to be mindful of time so that your meetings don't go way over the time allotted. However, sometimes it is necessary to spend more time and I believe that is OK. Again, the time spent working with the employee far outweighs the productivity lost in the long term because of the additional skills they would have gained if you're coaching correctly. If you're not a good coach or aren't working to develop those skills you might be wasting everyone's time. If that were the case I don't think you'd be reading this book in the first place!

Once we had covered any of their concerns as well as covered the items that I had on the agenda, the meeting would generally conclude with one more question from me and an action item for them. The question from me would be "do you have any other concerns that you want to bring up today?" This would give them a chance to bring up anything that may have come up for them during the conversation. I wanted to make sure they felt fully heard and all their concerns were addressed. I believe it's important for both building loyalty and trust in the leader as well as for overall performance that the employee feels taken care of. That final check-in is one of the ways to ensure this is done.

The action item at the end of the meeting is one that I wish I had learned much earlier in my career as a leader. It has become an integral part of my success and those I've taught it to. The final piece of the one on one meeting is to ask the question "what are your main takeaways from today's meeting?" Asking this question is important because it lets you know if they've taken away from the meeting what you intended. If not, you can clarify and if needed, even remind them of a topic covered if it was really meant to be one of the major takeaways. Once you've had them verbalize their takeaways the next step is to ask them to send you an e-mail with those takeaways. The e-mail is very important. Here's why…it solidifies in writing what was discussed. I recommend keeping a folder of the e-mails you receive back and referencing them in a future one on one. This also makes sure the employee can clearly communicate back what was discussed after you're no longer in the meeting room. If you get the e-mail back and it's completely different than what the intention of the meeting was, you can go follow up with them and clarify or coach again if necessary. Finally, it keeps a record of you doing your job. If you're ever asked by anyone you report to about your work, you can reference your coaching e-mails and provide progress updates on what's being done. You may experience a little resistance when you first ask for an e-mail back of the coaching session. That's not uncommon because it's different for most people. However, most of the employees I've worked with said they grew to appreciate sending the e-mail for the main reasons listed above. It kept them on track and focused on what they were needing to work on and were even able to reference the e-mails between meetings allowing them to do their own progress check. I've even had employees tell me that they continued with the practice of e-mailing takeaways even after they had moved onto a new leader that didn't ask for it because of how effective it was for THEM, not necessarily for their new leader.

Observation

Another method of coaching that is integral to achieving top performance is observation of the job being done. This can take many different forms and will be different depending on your industry or business. I'll begin with my experience as a sales leader primarily in a call center as well as share some firsthand stories of what coaching I received over the years as I was coming up as a new sales professional.

At this point I'll stop for a second to mention how important it is as an employee to just get some coaching in the first place. I can recall early on in my sales career that I didn't receive very much coaching…at least not from my supervisors. In the acknowledgements section I reference the first person that I can remember being coached by. He wasn't even one of my supervisors. He was a gentleman in his sixties that started with a company the same day as me. He had been in sales for many years while this was my

36

first real sales job. He would listen to me between his calls and give me tips and ideas on ways to improve my own sales. He also recommended books and programs to help me improve my sales. Upon reflecting, I received more coaching from Phil than I did from any of the six supervisors I had while working at that company. While I was successful there, had I received more guidance and coaching from my supervisors, especially as someone new to sales, I probably would have had much more success and the company would have benefitted.

After leaving that company I worked another sales job or two with mild success until I truly received coaching and saw the benefit that came with regular coaching for improvement. It came in the form of two siblings who worked for the company. Jared Burdick was the store manager at the store I worked at and his brother Nathan Burdick was the District Manager over the entire territory for wireless phone sales. What I admire most about the Burdick brothers was their willingness to roll up their sleeves and get their hands dirty. They talked the talk and walked the walk. Jared was not only the store manager, but he also was the top salesperson in the store. When he coached me on something it was easy to listen, especially because I was well aware based on his sales stats that he was better than me! Nathan was the same. Nathan rotated from store to store, but on the days that he worked with us in the store he was one of the top salespeople on any given day. He gave the sales he made to us in the store usually, having us do the order entry, which only made us even more loyal. He cared about us and had no problem helping us make money! One of the things that was consistent among both Jared and Nathan was that any time they had the opportunity to listen in while I was selling they would do just that. After the sales process was complete, whether it had resulted in a sale or not they would provide feedback on what I did well or any areas of opportunity throughout the interaction. I greatly appreciated their guidance and desire to help me grow and improve. I believe I grew as a sales professional more in the year and a half that I worked for that company under Jared and Nathan than I had in my previous six years in sales.

What Jared and Nathan did so well is what I'll call "observation and demonstration". As mentioned, they were there at every opportunity to listen in while I was selling. After observing they would then coach me on what I did well and what I could have done differently to close the deal. In some cases, if I was about to lose the sale, they would even jump in and help me end up getting the sale. Obviously, it was a benefit to the business overall and they gained something from it, but I also got to see a true professional in action. Afterwards they would ask me what I had learned by watching them after they had stepped in. This forced me to demonstrate my understanding of what they were doing differently than I had been doing that helped them close the sale. It also solidified in me what I had just learned.

The observation and demonstration approach that I learned while having Jared and Nathan as my leaders was my favorite and go-to method of coaching once I became a supervisor. While it was a slightly different environment, in person sales versus over the phone in a call center, the principles remained the same. In the call center setting you'll usually have many different tools at your disposal to observe. My preferred method was to observe the call live while the agent was on the call. Often, I would start out listening to the call without the agent ever knowing I was listening in. This way I could hear exactly how they approached the call when they didn't think anybody was listening. If the call was going fantastic I would not interrupt, instead opting to ask them what they thought about the call after the fact and then providing positive feedback on what to keep doing in future interactions. If the call was not going optimally, I would usually get on an instant messaging app and start typing in things for them to say. It's amazing how a call can turn around when the agent knows that the supervisor is listening in! Oftentimes, I would be jumping in not because it was a poor interaction, but because there was more that could be uncovered during the sales process to make a larger sale. I would type in additional questions for them to ask or even how to recommend a product and why. They would say it close to verbatim on the call and more times than not it resulted in a better sale than they were originally going to get or at least help close the deal in the first place. Not everybody enjoys this style of coaching, but over time as they got used to using the word tracks that I was feeding them to say it started to become second nature. When they were the top paid team in the call center that we worked in they didn't have any complaints. As a matter of fact, someone on another team once said to someone on my team that it didn't look like we ever had any fun...my team member told them that we actually had more fun than any other team because we had the money to do whatever we wanted outside of work and that when we were at work we were there to achieve big things! We were able to do that in large part due to what I learned while working with Jared and Nathan...observation and demonstration!

This doesn't have to be done just at the frontline level though! When I was a manager leading a team of supervisors, I took a similar approach to coaching. At least a couple of times a month I would go out to the supervisor's desk or station to simply observe for about an hour. In some instances, I wanted to watch an official coaching happen and at other times I just wanted to see how they approached their day to day duties while working with their team. This method gave us some of our biggest breakthroughs!

If the goal was just to observe them interacting with their team and how they coached on the fly, I would tell them to just go about their day like normal while I worked nearby. I would take notes on what I observed with the supervisor, how the team was functioning and anything else that I thought would be important to discuss with the supervisor. After the hour or so was up I would briefly meet with the supervisor to talk about what I had observed during that time. I always started off by sharing what I liked that they did, followed by anything that could be done differently to achieve greater results. Very similar to when I was coaching frontline agents and jumping in with an instant message to close more sales, if there was an opportunity I noticed that needed to be addressed right away I would jump in and help the agent myself or point out to the supervisor what they could do in that moment to help the agent and earn a greater sale.

The other way that I used this technique was when a supervisor had an official coaching planned. Typically, this meant going into a call observation room to sit down and listen to a call with the agent. I would go in with the supervisor and the agent explaining to the agent that I was there to observe the supervisor coach and that they were not in any type of trouble. You'll notice that many agents automatically think they're in trouble when the supervisor's boss is in the room. This is probably because few managers actually do this. By explaining your purpose, it helps to ease the agent's mind and make them more comfortable when there are multiple people in the room listening to their call. After observing the supervisor's interaction with the agent and how they coached, I took a three-part approach to the follow up coaching with the supervisor. Here are the questions I regularly asked...

What went well about the coaching that just happened?

If you had to do it again what would you do differently?

What are your takeaways from today's coaching session?

I always like to start with what went well or what they liked about the session. Most people automatically want to go to the opportunity, yet never recognize what was done well. In fact, when asked the question about what went well, many people will skip right over it and start talking about what they wish they would have done differently. You'll have to consciously stop them and bring them back to the positive before moving on. This is an extremely important aspect of a coaching observation! If all you're doing is pointing out things that didn't work well and ignore what did go right you're missing a huge opportunity to build up confidence and encourage the positive things you observed. Sometimes a person may not even recognize something they did that was fantastic, but by pointing it out you can ensure that they continue with that positive behavior in future coaching sessions.

If it was a newer supervisor without much experience in coaching employees, my approach was more direct. I would tell them flat out what I observed, what went well, what they could do differently and then make suggestions on what they should do in the future. If the supervisor was more tenured I took a more inquisitive approach, asking questions and leading down a path of self-discovery to what they could do during the interaction to create a better end result.

The final part of any coaching observation was the follow-up. I would ask them what their takeaways were from the session that we had just finished. I made sure to match up their takeaways with what I hoped they had gotten out of it. If it didn't match, I would make sure to revisit a topic if necessary. I always asked for an e-mail of what the takeaways were as well. The key is to then bring those takeaways to your next coaching observation to follow up on if they've made the key adjustments or are at least developing those skills and improving. It is a method that takes more work. You must be prepared for the coaching and sometimes it does take more time than just telling someone what they need to work on. I assure you that the time is well spent. You're making an investment in that person's future. They will learn and start to implement the tips and ideas you're giving them to improve. The result is a stronger overall leader with more tools to help the individuals on their team as well as helping the organization achieve greater growth overall!

Demonstration

Demonstration can take a few different forms. I've already referenced one of the ways that you can demonstrate while coaching by listening in and, when possible, showing how to get the job done. This will mean different things in different industries, but the concept is the same. Since we've already covered that method of demonstration, I won't go too much into it in this section.

The most obvious method of demonstration is to just roll up your sleeves and do the job yourself while the other person observes. This can be effective for those that are visual learners and need to see the job done first the right way, so they can duplicate it. An added benefit is that you are solidifying yourself as an expert and someone to be listened to, especially if you do the job better than the employee would normally do it themselves. This will happen often when you're working with newer employees and training them. If you have a more tenured team that is proficient in the work being done, you may need to use this method less often especially when working with frontline employees.

One of the ways that I've used demonstration in the past, and something I've found to be very effective, is what I'll call the reverse coaching observation. As a manager working with supervisors I would set up a coaching session where I would be the one coaching the sales professional with the direct supervisor observing the coaching session. I must admit, as someone who truly enjoys coaching, this was one of the most fun parts of the job for me. I would much rather be working with people and helping them improve rather than look at reports, send e-mails and just tell people what they should be doing. I'd much rather demonstrate!

During these sessions, typically we would go into a call observation room and start off by discussing whatever challenges the employee was facing. One of the questions I almost always asked of the employee was "when you leave this room, what do you hope to have gained from this coaching session?" Even if I already had a few things that I had planned on coaching on, I would tailor my entire session or presentation around what the employee wanted to get out of it. You'll find that people are way more receptive when they feel that it's their agenda you're working around than somebody else's. From there I would utilize any reporting that I felt would help further the conversation to support what the employee felt they needed to work on or show them that they may be doing better than they thought they were. It is important to build people up in these sessions as well by giving positive feedback as opposed to just talking about what they need to improve on. This approach will tend to make your employees more open to a coaching session in the first place. They won't feel that every session is designed to just give them "negative" feedback or things they need to work on. They'll come away feeling positive that they have received kudos for what they are doing well and actionable items that they can use to improve their performance in the future.

Oftentimes we would then listen to a recorded call from the agent with a specific focus on what they said they wanted to get out of the coaching while paying attention to any items that may have been identified that they were struggling with. The follow up always followed the same format, which should look familiar…

What did you like about the call or what went well?

If you had to do the call over again, what would you do differently?

What are your takeaways from today's coaching session?

I can't state enough the importance of starting with the positive. More times than not, I had written down far more positive things about the call than the agent did. I found this to be effective in setting up the session to be upbeat and making the employee feel safe. People are usually thrilled when you agree with them (if you do) on what went positive and then heap on a few more things that went well that they didn't even recognize themselves.

My coaching took a very sales-like approach. I frequently tied back what I was coaching on to what the employee stated they wanted to get out of the coaching session in the beginning. You'll often want to then role-play with

44

the agent after covering the topics, so they can see how what was covered will actually work when they're talking to a customer. I always ended with a question for the agent..." you said you wanted to gain (whatever they wanted) from today's coaching session. Do you feel like we were able to do that for you today?" If you've done a good job tying back your coaching to what they stated they wanted to get out of the coaching in the beginning, you'll rarely get any answer other than yes.

After the employee had left the room and I was just there with the supervisor, the coaching process would start all over again using the same questions reframed for the interaction. All coaching sessions ended the same way...with an ask for an e-mail of any takeaways they had from our time spent together. I found this to be a very effective method of demonstration. We were helping the frontline employee grow and become better, the supervisor was learning and developing new skills and I got to have the fun of frontline coaching which tends to get lost the higher up you move in a company.

Creating the Optimal Coaching Environment

One extremely important aspect of coaching is creating a "safe" environment for the coaching to take place. Think about it this way...nobody likes to feel like they are being judged, but in many cases a coaching session feels just like that! If the person being coached is in an emotional state of being nervous or fearful they are not going to get as much from the coaching as if they are in a positive, resourceful state of mind. Therefore, it's so important to maintain some level of consistency with your coaching sessions. Here, we'll go into a few ways that you can optimize your coaching sessions by setting up the environment.

While there are many different ways that a coaching can take place, as we've discussed earlier in this chapter, one thing that can help is setting an expectation prior to the coaching taking place. I found that scheduling the coaching session on the calendar so both me as the coach and the person that I was going to be coaching knew exactly when it was happening was very effective. This way it's not a shock to someone when their day gets interrupted for a coaching session. If they know the time they are going to be coached and it is on their calendar, it won't be a surprise. Another benefit for those who get nervous about being coached is that they can get themselves mentally prepared. I scheduled out my coaching sessions to the point where they were regular occurrences and put them out for as long as the employee had the schedule they were working. What ended up happening was that instead of employees being nervous about coaching, they would be excited! Often, if there was a time when I had to cancel, the person who was scheduled to be coached would ask if they could be rescheduled so that we could at least get some time in together before the next regularly scheduled session.

After you've scheduled out your formal coaching sessions, it is important to know what is going to take place during the session. Will this be an observation out in the field or will it take place at the office? If possible, this is something that can be helpful to add to the calendar invite so the person being coached knows what to expect. If the coaching is going to take place in the office, consistency with the location is important for both parties. Here's what I mean…if you're in a familiar setting you know how to access any tools that you'll need to use quickly. I've experienced times myself when I've had to coach in an unfamiliar office and couldn't pull reporting or tools up as quickly as I'd have liked. It caused the coaching session to go on longer than necessary and interrupted the flow of the coaching. For the person being coached, knowing the location and having it be consistent can be just as important. As human beings, new environments can be threatening. We also tend to associate certain environments positively and negatively. If the only time someone is brought to a certain room is when they're in trouble, they will automatically associate that room with something negative. I think this is one of the reasons that so many people don't like to be coached. Many supervisors will only pull an employee into a coaching room or give them time when something has gone wrong. If that's the only time you see a coaching room or go to the boss's office how can we expect someone to want to be there? If we are consistent with the setting of the coaching and are providing both positive feedback and feedback about the areas of opportunity it is much easier for the person being coached to feel good about that setting. If it's just as likely that they'll receive positive encouragement they'll be much more open and comfortable in the setting that you choose.

Structure

Another strategy that I utilize when coaching is to have a consistent structure to the coaching session itself. While I may not have a specific agenda when beginning the coaching, I tend to follow a format with every session. I've covered this briefly already in this chapter so here we'll do more of a review and outline that you can copy and print for your coaching sessions if you choose to.

- Greeting
- Opening
- Review
- Discussion
- Confirmation of Learning
- Conclusion
- Documentation

Greeting

The greeting is simple. This is welcoming the person being coached to the coaching session and attempting to set the tone. Since many people are nervous when they go into a coaching, the goal here is to start off the session in a positive tone, even if you have a tough topic to cover. I often kept a mini fridge in my office. It was not uncommon for me to offer the employee a water or soda, ice cold from the mini fridge. That small gesture helped to relax many people.

Opening

For the opening, I normally would spend time with some general small talk. I would use this opportunity to ask the employee about things going on in their life outside of work. I would follow up on any of their interests or fun things they had done recently. I used this as a way to further my knowledge of the individual, so I knew them a little more personally. This is mutually beneficial! You get to know the employee better and they also tend to relax a little more. When someone is talking about something they love or enjoy doing, it puts them in a positive state which makes the coaching go that much better. In this phase of the coaching I always like to ask the question "what would you like to get out of the time spent here today"?

Review

During the review we will begin with any takeaways they had from the last session and how they are doing with implementing or working on what was previously discussed. This is very important. If you coach, but never follow-up on what was coached on previously you are losing a major component that will lead to success. If someone receives coaching with no follow-up they may feel like there is no accountability and therefore not much of a reason to change their behavior.

In some cases, you may then continue with the previous takeaways if there is still work that needs to be done in that area. If not, now is the time to identify what will be covered during the current coaching session. This will then lead to an observation, call review, metrics review or just a general discussion of what needs to be improved on.

Discussion

Here is where the bulk of the time spent during the coaching session should take place. At this point, after you've done your review and determined the topic for the day, you'll do a deep dive into whatever you've agreed to discuss. I've learned that there are multiple approaches you can take during the discussion, but you need to gauge the level of your employee to determine which one you're going to take. If it's a newer or less experienced employee, I've found that being more direct is a better approach. Sometimes people just need to be told the most effective way to do something. This is especially true for the new employee who doesn't have much experience doing the work. You're more often going to just have to show and tell or demonstrate what needs to be done simply because they haven't seen as many scenarios as you have as the tenured leader. The other approach that I prefer to take is the "Pro-Coach" method. I learned this from a training by a company called ProSell based out of the United Kingdom. This approach relies on asking questions of the person being coached and having them walk themselves down a path that gets them to an answer. "Pro-Coach" is more like planting a seed for the employee and helping them figure it out themselves. The idea behind it is that people are more likely to do something when it's their idea as opposed to someone else's. What I love about "Pro-Coach" is that it truly helps to cement the idea for most people, especially because they're the ones that came up with it. As the coach, you just ask questions that lead them down the path to their own answer. I will issue a small warning here though…this approach has backfired on me when dealing with less tenured employees. If they truly don't know the answer or how to get to the desired outcome on their own, asking them questions can cause a lot of frustration. This is a technique that needs to be practiced, but once you master it you'll have much greater coaching sessions with more being retained by the employee.

Confirmation of Learning

No, this isn't a test however the confirmation of learning is one of the most important things you can do in a coaching session. If you skip this step it will set your coaching back and you may fail to cement what the person being coached was meant to get out of the session. Here's what you'll do and the reason why it works. At the end of the session simply ask for the three main takeaways that the employee got out of the coaching session.

Make sure that it aligns with what the goal of the coaching was in the first place. If you ask and they don't have anything that they took away, chances are that you didn't do a very good job of coaching. You may have covered things or told them that they need to improve in a certain area, but here's where you confirm that they are walking out with actionable items or tools that they can use to help them with that improvement. There are a couple of reasons that this approach works so well. One, is that you're very clear on if the desired objective with the coaching was achieved for both parties involved. If, as the coach, you find that your employees commonly have different takeaways than what was intended you know you have some work to do to improve your coaching delivery. Second, is that as your employees get used to you using this approach, you'll find that they are more engaged during the coaching. If they know they're going to be asked a question at the end and are expected to have takeaways they will usually end up paying more attention. The other piece is that you can now remind them that they clearly had the takeaways that were intended if there are further performance issues. Many employees will also come to the next session ready with their takeaways from the previous coaching to show their improvements in those areas.

Conclusion

Before wrapping up the coaching session I like to follow-up on the question that I asked during the opening. "At the beginning of the session you said that you'd like to get this and this out of today's coaching. Do you feel like you got what you were looking for today"? *Side note…when coaching I try to tie back what we are discussing to what they said they want to get out of the coaching session as often as possible. If I've done a good job with this, it is very rare for someone to leave the coaching feeling like they did not get out of it what they were looking for. * In almost every case the answer is yes, they did get what they were looking for. If the answer is no, I will revisit what they stated and tie back what we covered to what they wanted to get out of the coaching. If they still feel like they didn't get what they were looking for, which is extremely rare, I'll either take more time or acknowledge that there are some additional things they would like and that we'll make sure to devote the next session to covering those topics. The reality is that this happens so infrequently, but you must make sure you're doing a good job of tying things back to what they want to get out of the coaching session. The final piece to a good coaching, and something I wish I would have learned much earlier in my career in leadership, is to ask the employee to send an e-mail back with their main takeaways. Whenever possible, this should be done immediately upon the employee returning to their desk. It is helpful if you build time into the coaching for this to be done to ensure it gets sent back to you right away. Again, this is another way to solidify the coaching and what was discussed with the employee.

Documentation

In the corporate environments that I've spent much of my career in, you're not likely to get any disciplinary action approved by human resources unless you have solid documentation of what has been coached. I've even seen instances where it was clear an employee didn't care about the job and should be terminated for performance, but because there wasn't good documentation the employee was allowed to continue hurting the company with their poor attitude and performance. Documentation is not a fun part of the job of being a leader, but it is one that will benefit you the sooner you master it. There are various ways you can do this. One way is to take down all the notes yourself and keep them in a folder of some sort. I don't recommend you taking down your coaching notes during the coaching session with the employee because it can give off the perception that you're not paying attention to them. This makes for a poor coaching experience.

The best way to do this is by making sure you do something we've already discussed in this chapter. Have them send you an e-mail with what they took from the coaching session. Some companies have a tool to notate coaching, in which case it is extremely easy to copy and paste from the e-mail you received. If your company doesn't have such a system, all you need to do is create a folder for each employee in your e-mail program and save the e-mail from the employee in their specific folder. In addition to having great documentation (in the employee's own words even) it will make following up on what was previously coached that much easier.

This chapter is the longest in the book and for good reason. My belief is that a good leader spends most of their time coaching their employees. In this chapter we've discussed why good coaching is so important, different methods that can be used and a proven format for coaching success. Make the conscious effort to do right by your employees by spending the bulk of your time coaching them and helping them be successful. Not only will you inspire loyalty from those that report to you, you will truly be making your team and the organization overall better.

Chapter Five: Motivating

One of the most important things to remember is that everyone is motivated differently. Salespeople for example typically tend to be motivated by money. Studies have shown that most people are motivated by a sense of purpose or knowing that they are doing meaningful work. Others are motivated by fear of loss. Some are motivated by feeling they are a part of a team or something bigger. Still others are motivated by promotions or moving up in the company. It is critical that you find out what motivates the individuals on your team and what they respond best to.

Team Identity

One thing that has been consistent with the best teams that I've either been a part of or witnessed, is that they all had a sense of identity. This was created by the leader with the help of the team. The way that I've personally done this in the past is to set up a team meeting where I lay out my expectations and the identity I want for the team. I also ask the team what else we want to be known for. Through collaboration, we come up with the overall identity of the team. In addition to clearly defining the goals and objectives of the team I've also gone with the approach of selecting a name for the team. Practically all the top teams I've been a part of have done this. Sometimes the name is selected by the leader, sometimes the name just comes up organically and in other cases it's voted on by the members of the team. What's important is that you have a team name that everyone can rally behind. I've even gone so far as to have a logo created for the individual team! One of my favorite memories from my career is when my team of around one hundred and twenty people marched into a sales rally together chanting our team name. Everyone was blown away, including me because I didn't organize it! It's something that people even brought up fondly years later. I had people from other teams come up to me asking how they could get onto my team because obviously the people on the team were proud to be there and enjoyed what they were doing.

Motivating by Money

There are some people who aren't a fan of "motivating by money". For example, if the only way you can get someone to do something that's good for the business is by setting up an incentive you're training people to only go above and beyond when there's extra money in it for them. I agree that constantly throwing money at someone to get them to do something can be a bad thing. While it is one strategy, I don't think it's the best way to go for a business and it's actually NOT what I'm talking about when I say, "motivating by money".

What I am talking about is using what you know about people's financial desires, goals or even their current situation to motivate them to greater performance and potentially new heights financially. An effective method that I've used in the past is to first sit down with someone once they're new to the team. It's important to learn about them and what their goals are. My personal approach was to be up front and blunt about it…" what are your financial goals?" Or, through the course of the conversation and getting to know them I'll find something out about their life situation outside of work. It's then easy to tie back how making more money through their current position could help them better their life overall. Don't underestimate how powerful it can be to point out to someone that their life could be better and then show them the way to achieve it through hard work in your organization. I've had several people come back to me after they've accomplished something and thank me for taking the time to learn what was important to them and then show them how they could get what they wanted through hard work. I will admit that this is probably a little easier in a sales organization, but there are many ways you can use this in a position that isn't commissioned. Most companies offer end of year bonuses based on company performance. You can tie the individual's performance to how the company does at the end of the year and equate it to a better bonus payout. Typically, when someone gets promoted to a higher-level position, there is a pay raise that comes along with it. You can show them how their consistent, excellent work may result in a promotion. You can then easily show how the extra pay that comes with the promotion can help them achieve some of their financial goals. I certainly don't recommend motivating solely by money, however I do think it's an important part of motivation and a tactic that many people neglect to use.

Meaningful Work

People want to know that the work they are doing is making a difference. It's important that, as the leader, you are showing how the work being done is making a positive impact on the world or community you live in. It may take some creativity, but this is a very important part of motivating your employees. I'll use another example from my sales career here. I recall a time when I was working with an employee who was a phenomenal employee but wasn't getting the overall sales results that we needed of her. We sat down to discuss the challenges she was facing. I also spent some time observing her in action. Eventually, we got to the root of the problem which was that she felt like she was just ramming things down people's throats that they didn't need. A discussion ensued about what made her feel like the customers she was talking to didn't need the full spectrum of services that we offered. Her response was "well, they didn't call in about it in the first place". I asked her what services she had at home and she honestly replied that she didn't have everything that we offered. I then asked her to do a role play with me playing the part of the salesperson and her being the customer. I told her to answer me honestly just like in a normal conversation. Through asking her the right questions and learning about her family and household, I was able to position our full suite of services to her in a way that made sense based on the information she had given me. Even she agreed that she hadn't thought about our services in the way I had explained them and saw how having everything that we offered in her home could be very beneficial for her family. I asked her to think about how many customers may not be living as well as they could be because she neglected to even let them know about a product or service that we offered. That shift in mindset changed her way of thinking and got her to realize that the work she was doing actually DID make a difference and she could positively impact people's lives. From there her sales improved and she was still with the company for many years after that conversation.

Promotions/Moving Up

Employees who are looking to be promoted or move up can be some of the easiest to motivate. They already feel that their performance is top-notch, and in many cases, it is, or they wouldn't be looking to move up. For these employees I have found that giving them work that constantly challenges them is the best way to go. Look for special projects that won't hinder their current performance, but still allows them to take on new and exciting responsibilities. Show them how they can use the experience they gain from those special projects in future interviews to showcase their skills and ability to take on more work. If there aren't special projects to work on challenge them to beat their previous performance or set a new company record. As a teenager in the grocery business another employee and I were always scheduled to work the closing shift when the top store manager was scheduled to close the store. We found out that it was because we always got the closing work done the most accurate and fastest of anyone in our position. We took that as a challenge to get even better and see how fast we could get the end of night closing duties done while still producing top quality work. Word got out and eventually anyone that closed the store made it their goal to try and beat our quality of work and time. It ended up being a win-win for the store overall and it came about by the manager sharing with us that we were the best at closing duties.

Fear

A great leader that I had the pleasure of working with, James Buck III, used to say that some people are more motivated by the fear of loss than they are by what they'll gain. It is sad but true. Motivating through fear is my least favorite way to motivate. The unfortunate reality is that there are some people who are truly motivated best through fear. This is one of those places where I will go only as a last resort and typically only after the employee has proven to me that it's the best (or only) way that they'll be motivated. I know some managers use fear as their primary and sometimes only method of getting results. I personally don't think this is the best approach and here's why...people that are fearful will just work hard enough to not lose their jobs. They aren't people that are inspired and certainly won't go the extra mile. They'll do the minimum amount of work possible to stay employed and that's about it.

With that said, there are times where fear is a motivational tactic that you'll need to use. When I recognized that the only way I was going to get through to someone was through fear, I usually would then start looking for their replacement. This is because it is extremely rare for someone motivated primarily through fear to produce excellent results. If you're not in a position where you can replace the employee and need to use fear to get the desired outcome, here is what I'd recommend.

First, my hope is that you've already attempted all other methods of motivating in order to create an inspired employee as opposed to a fearful employee. If that hasn't worked, my approach would be to sit down with the employee and review previous coaching conversations. Remind them of what has already been talked about and what has been done to try and give them the skills and motivation to achieve the necessary results. This sets you up to not be "the bad guy", but as someone who has tried everything they can think of to help the employee succeed. From there the conversation can shift to whatever performance challenges the employee is still facing followed by another reminder of what has previously been done to help them be successful. Finally, after reviewing the key performance metrics and what coaching has already taken place the conversation can shift to the future consequences of continuing to not meet performance expectations. This is where the fear comes in. It may be fear of getting a corrective action or write-up or it could even be the fear of completely losing their job. Either way you've set clear expectations, shown what has been done to try and help the employee and then communicated that future failure could lead to formal corrective action or even termination of employment. My experience has been that while this may gain you some additional time of acceptable performance, in most cases the employee will return to old habits and you'll end up having to part ways. I can personally only think of one time where I had to motivate by fear where the employee responded positively and was appreciative. There are always exceptions to the rule!

You cannot become a great leader without learning how to properly motivate the people that you lead. I believe this to be true not only in business, but also in family life! The most important aspect of motivation is in not motivating others by what motivates you, but by finding out what truly motivates them. Too many people try and take a "one size fits all" approach to motivation which simply does not work. Learn the individual, create a team identity that they can get behind, find out what's important to them inside of and outside of work to positively motivate them and use fear only after you've exhausted all other options.

Chapter Six: Using Reporting to Manage

The 50 Billion Dollar Man, Dan Pena said "what gets measured gets accomplished". I absolutely believe this to be true. Plus, if it's coming from someone who has helped create $50 billion in revenue I would say its sound advice to follow. For anyone that has worked in a call center before you know that virtually everything is measured. In most sales organizations there are many different types of stats that are looked at to see what is contributing to the success and growth of the company. I even recall that when I was working in the grocery store we had a tracking system for how many items were rang up per cashier. Utilizing your organization's data to help you lead your team is critical to the long-term success of your team and the company itself.

I have worked with supervisors who just "went with their gut" when leading their teams. Sometimes they were right and sometimes they weren't. I think that's the problem with failing to use all your resources when leading. While you may not always be right even when using the data to guide you, you'll find that you're right more often than not when you're using all the information at your disposal to help you make decisions and lead your team. I've even seen examples where companies get to the brink of failure because the people in leadership positions were ineffective at interpreting and using the data to help guide the company to long term success.

One of the first things you'll want to do when you move into a leadership role or start a new position is to figure out and learn the tools available to help drive performance. Notice that I write, "tools you have to help drive performance". I've seen times where supervisors or managers spend all their time JUST looking at the numbers or tools all day long and never actually get any real work done. Sure, they're busy, but they're not actually driving any performance because they're hiding behind their desks looking at the numbers all day. So, find out what your key metrics are and then find what tools you can use to help you drive those metrics. Once you've determined this, your focus should be on utilizing those tools that will help you ensure top performance.

What has always worked for me and what I'd recommend doing is setting up a schedule for what reporting you're going to run and when. There are going to be some metrics that you'll want to watch every day and there are others that, while still important, are things you'll only need to use on a weekly or monthly basis. Determining which reports are daily, which are weekly, and which are monthly can help you to avoid the trap of looking at reports all day and not actually accomplishing anything. Once you've determined the reporting you're going to use on a daily basis, you'll want to begin using those tools first thing in the morning to help guide how you're going to approach the day. Analyze the previous day, week or month to determine where your time is going to be best spent and where you're going to make the biggest impact for your business. Using the call center environment as an example you may be looking at overall call time for the previous day or week. If you have a team or individuals who are outside of where they need to be, you know that you'll want to put some focus into those teams or individuals to get their call times in line. You may spend a half hour looking at the data, but if you use it correctly and allow the data to show you where you need to focus your day, you can make huge positive impact to your business results and bottom line. Far too many people go into the day without a plan and then hide behind looking at data and reports to make it look like they're doing something. At the end of the day the results you achieve is what matters the most so take time to utilize your reporting, but don't be the person that hides behind them in order to not actually do any work.

Learning and then utilizing your tools and reporting methods is one of the most important things you can do as a leader who is looking to achieve top performance. Set up a schedule to prioritize what metrics you'll want to look at daily, weekly and monthly and then use that data to help you guide your team to success. Setting up a schedule will help you avoid falling into the trap that plagues some people of pulling and staring at reports all day without truly accomplishing anything. Reporting is extremely important to the health of a business when used the right way so make sure to use your resources correctly to grow your team and overall results.

Chapter Seven: Hiring Right

One of the toughest, yet most important parts of being a leader is hiring correctly. There are few things as critical to the success of your business as bringing in the right people to your organization. You want to bring in people that will work hard, are coachable, bring the right skills and fit your team or company culture. This is much easier said than done. Where I've personally seen the best results are in those organizations where the leader is hiring directly for their own team. I believe this is important because the leader made the decision to bring the person on and is directly responsible for that person's growth and development. If the employee doesn't work out for some reason, the leader who made the hiring decision is then able to grow and learn from their decision. This helps to develop the leader and it also results in a better organization overall because the people bringing in new employees develop their hiring skills and bring on people who are the best fit for the business and for their team. I've seen organizations where the people making hiring decisions never actually had the people they hired directly report to them. Sometimes they never even interact with the new employee again after making the hiring decision in the first place! To me, this is a huge mistake.

Why is building the right team so important? Aren't there many people capable of doing a job? The honest answer to that is yes, there are many people who can do the job. Will they do it in a way that supports the team or organization's objectives? Maybe and maybe not. Therein lies the problem with just hiring the first person you interview that can do the job.

I know there are people out there who will read this and say that it opens the door for discrimination. While that may be correct if a hiring decision is being made to not hire someone based on factors such as race, age, sexual orientation or any other protected class, that's not what I'm talking about here. My guess is that people who would say you should hire the first person that is capable of doing the job have never built a team or been held responsible for their hiring decisions. As someone who has been involved in probably thousands of interviews and hundreds of hiring decisions I know there's more to getting the job done than just doing the work. This is the reason it is so important for the success of an organization to build the right team.

Allow me to expand on this with some of my experiences related to building a team. I've worked with organizations where we seemingly did hire simply based on if a candidate could do the job or not. While that sounds great on paper and made it very easy for the person doing the interview, it rarely led to the best results. The reason for this is that there is a huge difference in someone being able to do a job and somebody truly wanting to do the job. If you're setting your team or organization up for success don't you want people that are excited for the work that they're doing? A real-life example of this that I've personally witnessed is someone being hired for a sales role that didn't even really like sales!

You certainly don't want a team where everyone is alike either. You don't even want a team full of people that you want to go and hang out with after work! If everyone is the same and thinks alike it will lead to less creativity and ultimately lower results. What you're truly looking for is a diverse group of people with skills that complement each other. So, if you're not just looking to hire the first person that can do the job what are you looking for?

First, it's important to clearly define what your goals are. Like the example above, if you're hiring for sales you can't expect to get the best results when you hire someone that doesn't really like sales in the first place. Similarly, if you're hiring for a customer service role why would you ever hire someone that doesn't bring personality and a positive tone to the interview? Chances are good that they're going to have the same tone when working with a customer. Can they do the job? Sure. Will they do it in a way that you want to have your company represented? Probably not! Look to hire the people that bring the best qualities to the role that you're filling.

Next, it's important to look at your team holistically to determine what you're missing. I know that some of my areas of opportunity are fun and creativity. For me to build the best team that will get the best possible results, I need to look to hire people that are strong in the areas of fun and creativity. The same concept applies if you have a team full of people that are fun and creative. You'll want to mix it up and hire someone that may be more results and goal-oriented.

Finally, look to your values and the values of the organization when making a hiring decision. While you do want to hire people with different strengths to lift the team overall, the one constant should be values. If some of your core values are honesty and integrity you should be keying in on those areas during the interview to ensure the candidate shares those same values. I personally love competition. When I'm interviewing someone for my team I want to make sure that they are also a competitive person. This is the reason I say it's so important to build the right team. Again, there are many people in the world who can do a job. If your values are not aligned with the people you are bringing into the organization, it will do more harm than good. People on the team won't work as well together or get along at work because they aren't aligned in terms of their values. Some of my favorite teams I've worked with were the ones where we were all very different in terms of personalities, traits and skills but had similar values. Conversely, some of the most challenging teams I've worked with were less diverse overall but were vastly different in terms of values.

If you're in a position where you're hiring for your own team you want to make sure that you're learning from your hiring successes and mistakes. The first person that I ever hired for my own team was a phenomenal person and a great worker. She even did a good job taking and applying feedback. However, while she had previous sales success in another industry and said that she loved selling, she did not enjoy closing. She was uncomfortable applying any pressure when someone was not ready to decide right away. I didn't know this until after I had hired her on to be a part of my team. She ended up leaving the company to take a job with less sales pressure required. The lesson I learned from the experience was to ask more questions about a person's background and what they enjoyed and didn't enjoy about previous work. This learning experience helped me greatly over the years as I continued to build my team. If you want to be successful in building your team one of the best things you can do is to track and analyze the results of your hiring decisions. In doing so you will grow as a leader in selecting and developing talent which will grow the business long term.

So, what makes a good hire? That really comes down to the organization and the job itself. Someone who loves customer service but thinks it's poor customer service to encourage someone to make a buying decision is probably not going to be a good fit for your sales organization. On the same hand, someone who values freedom and working on their own schedule isn't going to be a good fit for a very structured call center environment. A person with all the technical knowledge in the world but poor communication skills probably won't be a good fit for a customer facing IT role no matter how good they are with fixing computer problems. One of the reasons I think it's important for the hiring manager to make the decision of who's going to be hired onto their team is because a good hire can also mean something different to one person than another. I've personally seen cases where it appears on paper that a candidate is a perfect fit for a position. There are times when, due to personality and communication differences in who they end up reporting to, the person who looked like they'd be a perfect fit failed miserably. In this case, I don't necessarily think it's anybody's fault. However, I do believe that if you're seeing this in your organization, the decision makers should assess how employees are hired and on-boarded.

I truly believe that it is imperative that you look for the best people for the job that is going to be done and structure your interview questions in a way that helps you identify that best candidate through the interview process. There are some things that are red flags and would be almost definite deal breakers for me. These would include:

Talking negatively about a previous employer.

Not being able to answer the question being asked, especially if opportunities have been given to clarify.

Failing to prepare for the interview at all.
Cursing or using unprofessional language during the interview.
Failing to arrive on time for the interview.
Negativity in general.

I would also recommend that you check in with your receptionist or front desk staff prior to making your ultimate hiring decision. See how they were treated by the candidate before being interviewed. How they treat the front-desk staff is often an indicator of how they will treat their co-workers. You want to bring in people who will not only perform at a high level but will also be uplifting for your organization.

Hiring right is critical to the success of a business. To ensure the greatest levels of success the person making the hiring decision should have the person they've hired report to them. Identify what is most important to the business and structure your interview questions around finding the person with the qualities that match. Be on the lookout for red flags or anything that would indicate a poor fit for the organization. Utilize the advice of your front-desk staff as well to find out how the candidate acted prior to the interview and get an idea of how they'll interact with co-workers once they are hired. After considering all factors involved, then make the decision on if the candidate is the right fit for both the job and the company.

Chapter Eight: Recognition

Everybody craves recognition. Sure, there will be some people who will tell you that they don't care but the reality is that they want to be recognized in some other way. Maybe it's even just being recognized that they don't do well with traditional recognition. There are few things you can do to ensure a successful team that are as powerful as real, meaningful recognition for a job well done. My philosophy has always been to recognize as often as possible!

Don't get me wrong, it's not always easy to provide recognition. Sometimes you have to look for reasons to recognize someone when it comes to performance. There are even those who feel like they shouldn't have to recognize an employee when they're just doing their job or that the money paid to the employee should be enough recognition on its own. I happen to disagree with that approach. In this chapter I'll share some of the strategies that I've used over the years, and continue to use, to create a positive culture where performance is recognized.

Name Recognition

I stated earlier that it's not always easy to recognize people. I will have to admit that I was a little off with that statement in one regard. It is always easy to recognize people using one of the things they hold most dear to them. Dale Carnegie said, "remember that a person's name is to that person the sweetest and most important sound in any language". I believe you should make it a point to know the name of every person on your team. Surely this will be easy for small teams. In the case of a small team I would go one further as to learn something about the individual as well. This isn't quite as easy when you've got hundreds of people that directly or indirectly report to you, but with some work it can be done. When, through team changes, new people began reporting to me one of the first things I would do is ensure name tags were put up at the desks of my employees. I would go around each morning as the shift started and each evening when the shift ended to acknowledge each employee. It normally only took me about a week of this routine before I knew the name of everyone on my team and was able to address them by name when I saw them in the hall or even outside of work. More than once I was told how meaningful this was to people. They said that other managers they had didn't take the time to learn their name or know who they were. The fact that I knew who they were made them want to work even harder and that it was clear that I truly cared about them.

Birthdays

I mentioned this one earlier in the book, but another relatively easy way to recognize people is to save their birthday in a calendar and then either tell them happy birthday or do something special for them. One of the ways I did this was to buy a birthday cake for the individual and serve it to the team when it was someone's birthday. It was a fun and lighthearted way to build camaraderie while recognizing a team member for something that was special to them. As I took on roles where I was leading leaders, I would take the team out to lunch whenever possible to celebrate a birthday. Again, it was a way to get the team together outside of work and recognize someone publicly. The cost was usually around $100 but the value far outweighed the money that I spent!

Top Performance

One of my favorite ways to recognize is through performance trophies. Determine what metrics are important to your organization and then go out and buy a traveling trophy or two that goes to the top performers for the day, week or month. I had a professional wrestling championship belt for the top overall monthly performer, a toy ATM that shot out fake money for the person with the highest overall revenue and a toy monster truck for the person with the most overall production. They were inexpensive, yet fun ways to show appreciation and recognition for a job well done. It was not uncommon for people to take pictures with their trophy and post it on their Facebook or other social media page. Ideas for other industries may be a plush heart for the employee with the highest customer satisfaction scores or a toy scanner for the grocery store checker with the most products scanned per hour. Have fun with it and be creative!

Not every company will have the budget to do this, but if you do I recommend either an annual or quarterly incentive in the form of a trip or day off. Some of the best performance I've ever seen was when someone was striving to reach a goal of a trip that the company was offering. They'd work overtime, work just a little harder than they might normally, or even ask for feedback to help them make long term improvements in the quest to win the trip. Some of the things I've seen done in the past are trips out of state sponsored by the company, airline vouchers for the employee to take their own vacation when they wanted to and local beach trips for those of that live near a coast. Other ideas could include a paid day off with a gift certificate for a spa day or tickets to a sporting event.

Improvement

It's not uncommon to have an employee who isn't doing very well in their role for one reason or another. This is still an opportunity for positive recognition. When they do make improvements make sure to celebrate the improvement. You might do this in public or in private with just the employee alone. Either way, it's important to make sure that they know they have improved and that you appreciate the improvements that they've made in their role. If possible, my recommendation would be to make it a public recognition. This way the entire team sees that you as the leader not only appreciate top performance, but you also appreciate when effort is being put in to make improvements. People will work harder when they know that the work they do is meaningful and appreciated so make sure to show it when someone has improved.

Recognition is a huge motivator for people. There are many ways that you can recognize your employees for a job well done. The most important thing is that you do it! Use some of the ideas from this chapter or come up with your own. By reinforcing good behaviors with recognition, you will gain greater results for your organization and the respect of your employees. A memorable experience for me was when I once heard a top performer say with tears in their eyes "I just wanted to be told I was doing a good job by [the CEO]". That CEO wasn't strong in the area of recognition and the result was we lost what had previously been one of the top performers in the company. That could have been avoided had the right behaviors been reinforced and nurtured through positive recognition. I can't say enough how important it is that you take the time to recognize your employees for a job well done.

Chapter Nine: Managing for Results

In a sales environment, one of the most important things you can do to lead your team to success is to know the commission plan inside and out. You'd be surprised at how many sales leaders don't do this. As a matter of fact, it wasn't something that came naturally to me either. I learned it by watching another leader work with his team. I was in a situation where I was basically an assistant manager on a team that, when I joined, was consistently ranked last place. Fortunately, I was seated next to a leader with a consistently top performing team. I knew that I had a lot to learn so anytime they had a team meeting in their area I would take the time to listen to what they were covering during the meeting. I found that they consistently talked about the commission plan and how to maximize the plan. They talked sales strategy, overcoming objections and closing, but ultimately, everything came back to how to make the most amount of money by selling to the structure of the commission plan. Naturally, I adopted this best practice! By the time I was promoted to run my own team, the team that I was the assistant manager for had gone from being a consistently last placed team to one that was consistently finishing in the top two. Looking back, I'm actually glad that I didn't learn this tactic until later in my sales career. Had I truly known how to sell to the commission plan early on, I would have made way more money at multiple companies. I may not have wanted to take the pay cuts that I ended up taking to move into leadership roles had I been making a larger income than I was already making at that time.

There are multiple benefits to utilizing this as a leadership strategy.

Employee Retention

In my experience, paid employees are happy employees. When employees know the commission plan and know how they're paid they tend to be happier, provided that we as the leaders are then helping them develop the skills to maximize that commission plan. When employees don't know the plan or how they get paid, they are wandering aimlessly just trying to sell anything possible. In business, we know that there are certain objectives that help the company grow. In most cases the commission plan is designed to more significantly reward selling products that help the company grow (and if they're not, the commission plan should be changed to support the business objectives). We must help our employees understand how they are paid and why they are paid different commissions for the various products or services that help the business grow. By doing so, we are in turn backing up the value of the company's product offerings. Employees want to feel that the work they are doing is making a difference. Through explaining to them the benefit to the customer, the company and possibly most importantly the employee themselves, we are clearly showing them how their work is making a difference. In addition, if the commission plan is backing up the business objectives and we are teaching them how to effectively sell to the plan, we are decreasing the likelihood that we'll have to performance manage or terminate employment due to sales. If we as the leaders have done a good job of helping our team maximize the plan, there will be trust that we will be able to do the same thing should business objectives or the commission plan change in the future. This helps to reduce turnover of our top people, who are generally never happy when there is a change to the way they are paid. Retaining top employees typically leads to what we see next...

Increased Results

As long as the commission plan and the business objectives are properly aligned, managing to the commission plan is one of the best things you can do to support the business. If you are teaching your team exactly how to get results that are congruent with the structure of the commission plan you are naturally going to have a top performing team. This is because everything they do is in line with supporting the needs of the organization.

First, I'll use an example of when this wasn't done well in my past. I was working as a sales associate at a company selling wireless phones. This was before unlimited data plans and the smart phones that we have today. I think the hot phone at the time was the Motorola Razr for those of you that remember that far back. In that commission plan it was heavily structured to the primary new line of service. Lines added on as part of a family plan paid a much smaller amount to the business and people who upgraded their phone or extended their contract paid the sales associate at a much lower commission rate. The service that paid a fairly large percentage but was not promoted in the store I worked at was the data plans that were available. Granted, while the phones back then didn't have nearly the capabilities that the phones of today have, it was still a neat and truly useful feature if presented properly. The focus in the store was completely on new activations-and while there was a tier system that paid more per new activation with each tier the sales associate achieved-it was not the only way to make money with the commission plan. Looking back, I'm not sure if the new activations aspect of the plan was promoted so heavily because that's how the owner or store manager made money or if there were other factors involved. Had my leader at the time (who I did and still do consider to be a fantastic leader) truly focused on the ways that we could have made more money as sales associates in the store we would have increased our average revenue per sale. The result would have been greater overall store revenue through each sales associate maximizing each opportunity that we were presented with when someone visited the store. Whether the customer came in to activate a brand-new line, upgrade or renew an existing line of service or even just a customer service opportunity we would have been focused on adding revenue instead of just looking for the new activation.

A time when I utilized this strategy with my team and it worked out perfectly to support the business objectives was when I took over a consistently underperforming late shift team in a call center. Most of the sales associates that were working that schedule were there because they had less than stellar results and were bid into the late shift because higher performers took the "good shifts" earlier in the day. A lot of the employees wanted to make excuses as to why they couldn't perform like the day shift or how it was unfair that they were stuck working the "tougher" late shift. Having worked the late shift as a sales associate when I first started with the company, I knew that while there were certain challenges to the later shift, there were also certain benefits. One of my primary objectives when I took over that team was to show people how they could make money by selling to the commission plan through making some simple adjustments to how they approached their calls. First, I had to make sure that everyone understood what the commission plan was and how it worked. I gathered up all the supervisors that reported to me at the time and went through the plan with them to ensure their understanding. I also made sure that they were aware of how they were paid and that helping their teams make more money would in turn make them more money as well! I then had each supervisor deliver what the commission structure was and how to maximize it during a team meeting. From there we had to acknowledge the differences between the later and earlier shifts. We talked about the unique challenges of each shift and how working late could be advantageous in certain situations. Between the supervisor and I, we trained on how to recognize and then capitalize on those situations where the late shift had the advantage. As this was an inbound call center, we also spoke about people's tendency to call into the sales department regardless of what department they were trying to reach simply to get ahold of a live human being. I know, we all do it. We talked about how to quickly identify the sales opportunity, while still kindly addressing the initial reason for the call and then determining if there was a sale to be made. After attempting to address their concern we would then transition into seeing if there was an opportunity to help the customer through our other products and services. If we determined that it was something that would be better served through another department we would kindly transfer them to an expert that was better trained to service that particular issue. In many cases, we found that we were able to help them with their concern and then utilized that opportunity to educate the customer on our products and services that they may have been missing out on. Another area that had been a challenge for the later shift was higher than average use of hold and unproductive time after the call had ended. The late shift tended to get fewer calls than the earlier shift already so there was no room for any unproductive time. This was a huge focus of myself and my team of supervisors. By using the approach of explaining how the commission plan worked and identifying the unique aspects of the shift being worked we were able to bring unproductive time to the lowest in the call center. We were still able to keep our overall call times in line with the earlier shifts due to our focus on maximizing each call. While we didn't finish at the top, we did achieve in about six months the best results, both sales and operationally, the later shift had ever accomplished.

Happy Employees

While this certainly ties in with increased employee retention, I'm going to categorize it separately. Maybe I'm doing this selfishly and breaking it out into its own category because it's one of my favorite parts about being a leader.

I gain a huge amount of personal satisfaction when an employee that I've worked with to grow, develop and support comes to me to let me know about something great they're doing in their life. When you have employees that know the commission plan and are able to maximize it, they are going to be some of the top paid people in your company. When people know exactly how they need to do their job to earn what they need to achieve their financial goals outside of work, they don't dread coming to work anymore. They come in with a sense of purpose. They know what they need to earn to get that new car or buy that house or even take that family vacation. They're happy and excited to get to work each day knowing what they need to do. Without providing that direction, people will wander aimlessly. Sometimes they'll get good results and a good paycheck and other times they may not and will be stressed out and worrying about if they're going to be able to keep their job. That's not a fun way to live...believe me, I've done both. One of my favorite experiences was when someone who had reported to me sent me a message. It said, "I just got preapproved for a mortgage. We are going to start seriously looking at buying a house". The most powerful part about it for me was that the individual mentioned that he could trace back his decision to start the process of buying a home to a conversation that him and I had earlier in the year about his goals and what he would need to do sales wise to achieve them. He thanked me for giving him the push that he needed. That's the kind of thing that creates a happy employee, wouldn't you agree?

If you're in a position where you are the one that creates the commission plan, always look to make sure it aligns perfectly with the business objectives. This way there are no mixed messages or confusion. Those that want to succeed and make the most money will ultimately be aligned with doing what's best for the business. While this seems like a natural way to run a business, I have seen it firsthand where the commission plan and the business objectives weren't aligned, with the right people not being rewarded.

These concepts still apply even in a non-commissioned environment. As the leader you just need to make some simple adjustments in your approach. Instead of focusing on the commission plan, focus on how to maximize any quarterly or yearly bonuses your team may receive. More importantly, focus on what your employees will do with their bonus and encourage them to print out something that helps them see what they can achieve through hard work.

Not every company pays out bonuses for performance, even though I think they should! Let's say your company doesn't pay performance bonuses. Talk to your employees about their aspirations and how strong performance or skill improvements can help them achieve what it is that they want to achieve both inside and outside of work. Show them what an excellent performance review may end up looking like for them in terms of a raise or even a promotion. Then, tie it all back to what they'll be able to accomplish in their personal lives as a result of that pay raise or promotion.

As leaders, whether in a commissioned environment or not, by helping the people that report to us earn more money we can make a lasting impact in their lives and the lives of their families. I've seen this in action with leaders who do manage to the commission plan or bonus structure and leaders who do not manage to the commission plan or bonus structure. In every case that I can remember, the leader who did manage to the commission plan or bonus structure and helped their employees earn more money had overall happier and more productive employees who ended up staying with the company.

Chapter Ten: Performance Management

Ah, the dreaded performance management! Performance management aka accountability and discipline is one of the toughest things to do even for tenured leaders. That's because it's hard and certainly no fun. I've only met two people in my entire career who actually enjoyed this aspect of the job…and there are times when I've questioned their sanity! For most people performance management, and especially terminating someone's employment, is extremely uncomfortable. While at this point in my career I've had to performance manage and terminate employment for more employees than I'd like to admit, it is still something that causes a tinge of nervousness for me when having to do it. However, I wish I would have gotten good at it or at least improved my skills in this area when I was new as a leader. The truth is that it is a necessary part of being a good leader. It's not fair to you, your team or your organization to keep people employed that aren't good for the business and aren't making the effort to improve. I am all for giving people chances. Throughout the years I've probably given people too many chances! Part of that comes down to the fact that I just wasn't comfortable and didn't know the right way to performance manage effectively. In this chapter I'll share some of the lessons that I've learned over the years and tips on making performance management easier for you when it's something you must do.

We touched on this in the last chapter, but one of the first things you need to do if you want to truly be effective with performance management is to have some sort of system that you use to track your coaching and employee performance. This is very true in the corporate setting, but even if you're a small company, having something in place where you're documenting the coaching session will be a great benefit to your business. At the very least it could help you avoid a discrimination lawsuit and all the costs associated with that. I laid out my favorite method of documentation in the last chapter, but I've also seen leaders effectively use Excel, web-based tools and even good old pen and paper with a filing cabinet to document. Whichever method you use is fine…just make sure to use one!

It's also important to make sure that your employees are clear on not only what is expected of them, but the consequences of failing to meet those expectations. In most of the companies I've worked with there has been a clear progression path for those that are not meeting the job requirements although there are certain offenses that could take someone straight to termination of employment.

The approach to performance management that I've found to be best is really quite simple. It involves just a few steps and doesn't need to be nearly as uncomfortable as most make it out to be. Again, this is something I developed over time and it was certainly not something I was good at right out of the gates. If you've been coaching and documenting correctly it won't come as a huge surprise to the employee when you do have to meet about their performance. I've found it helpful to start off by reviewing the conversations you've already had about the performance issue. It shows that you've put in the work to try and help the employee be successful and reminds them that you're not just writing them up because you feel like it. It is something that has been worked on, coached to, documented and the performance still has not improved. At that point, performance management is just the next logical step. When approaching it this way, you'll find that very rarely do you get push back from the employee. Sure, they are disappointed, but they understand that it is necessary after seeing all the work that has been done to try and help them improve.

Once you've reviewed the conversations that have been had, it is now time to review the performance metrics briefly to show how performance has fallen short. This is important because most people still don't want to believe that their results have been that bad. Even after reviewing the conversations and documentation, I've still had people who were surprised when I've showed them the performance metrics detailing how they've failed to meet expectations. I had one person tell me "well, when you look at it like that I guess we have to move to the next step." They didn't want to be written up for their performance, but they completely understood after having it all laid out for them.

At this point you've reviewed the coaching that has taken place and the performance that has essentially not taken place. The next step is to just be confident and direct, and let the employee know that based on their performance so far it is going to have to result in a write-up or corrective action. Early on in my career as a leader, I felt the need to apologize for writing someone up. I came to the realization that there is no need to apologize! In every case where I had to write someone up I gave them every chance to improve. As I learned how to more effectively performance manage, it was more common to have the employee apologize to me for having to write them up! Using this method that I've outlined above it just becomes so clear, even to the employee, that they will usually accept responsibility for what has to happen.

Even as you're having to write someone up, it is important to remain positive and optimistic. I remember a quote from a great leader I worked with, James Buck III, where he said, "it's only a problem if you plan on doing it again." He would say this almost every time he had to write someone up. I loved it and started using it myself because it was a reminder that this doesn't have to happen again. The circumstances can change, and the employee can choose to improve their performance and not be in this position in the future.

The next step is to work with the employee to game plan how to avoid being in this position in the future. Even though you will have already done this in past coaching sessions, you'll find that after someone gets written up and there is official documentation they tend to take things more seriously. Whereas before they may have taken it as just coaching and not made any changes, now that there is a chance their job is on the line they may take some positive action to improve their performance. This step in the process is designed to keep things moving forward and give the employee hope that they can change and get themselves out of their current situation. I can't say how many times I've had to write somebody up and once it was done their performance drastically changed for the better. This is what really helped me understand that performance management is not a bad thing. For some people it's what they need so that they can realize that changes need to be made to the way they are doing things. If all it takes is them signing a piece of paper to make the necessary adjustments to improve then they could have done it all along. The moment I realized this is when I no longer looked at performance management in a negative light.

The final piece to the performance management puzzle is the documentation. In many cases this is something that you'll have a formal document in place already and have gotten approval from Human Resources. If that's the case in your organization then your documentation is already taken care of. You'll want to offer the employee a copy of the paperwork as well. Some will turn it down, but others are motivated by it. I recall an employee who profusely apologized to their supervisor for putting them in the position to having to write them up. They then took the corrective action paperwork and posted it at their desk as a reminder of what they needed to do to improve. The employee used that as motivation, made the necessary changes and was a productive employee for years after with no other performance issues. If you don't have an official document, I recommend you use the documentation method outlined in the last chapter and have the employee send you an e-mail with their takeaways from the meeting and what they are going to do to improve their performance.

Terminating an Employee

Terminating employment for somebody is one of the most difficult parts about being a leader. Early on in my career, when I had to terminate an employee I felt like I had failed them as a leader. That's not necessarily the case. If you have done everything you could to help them grow and develop and they still do not improve, it really isn't your fault and you're just doing what is a natural part of being a leader. Some supervisors, especially those that are new in their role, will shift the blame to the company or the human resources department as the one ultimately making the decision. Even I was guilty of doing this as a new leader. This is the wrong approach to take. You are the leader and are most likely the one presenting the facts to human resources for the decision to be made to terminate the employee. Take responsibility for what needs to be done. You don't necessarily have to say, "I made the decision", but you shouldn't put the blame on anyone else either. In all honesty, employees talk to each other and how you handle the meeting will get back to others on your team. If you come across weak and place the blame on the company or your HR department, it will get out to the rest of your team members. Be the strong leader that you are and know that what you're doing is in the best interests of you, the company and in most cases the employee being terminated themselves.

I can't recall the first termination meeting that I had to conduct. What I do recall is the emotion that came with having to terminate an employee for at least the first few years of me being a leader. My hands would get sweaty, I would stammer when talking, my heart would race, I would feel like I had to go to the bathroom…basically a lot of the symptoms that come with having a panic or anxiety attack! It's no fun!

I am a process person so after multiple episodes of what I described above when having to lead a termination meeting, I decided that I needed to figure out a better way. I ended up with a system that kept me on track throughout the meeting and allowed me to look at a visual if I did find myself getting flustered or having those feelings of anxiety and panic.

Here's the process that I used, which helped me out immensely, and I hope it also helps you with this very difficult component of being a leader. First, I would write down on a sheet of scratch paper how I envisioned the meeting going. For example, I would write how I would introduce the meeting. In most cases there had been some form of an investigation or coaching that had occurred with the employee prior to the termination meeting. I may jot down some of the facts, so I could review them during the meeting. Once I had written down what I felt I needed, I would position it somewhere that I could quickly look at during the meeting if I needed to. The next step for me was visualizing how the meeting would go. In these types of stressful situations, my mind seems to automatically want to go to the worst possible scenario. I would force myself to think only about how the meeting would go positively, despite the difficult subject matter. This caused me to only visualize positive outcomes. Not surprisingly, after I started doing this, most of the meetings did end up going as well as a termination meeting can go!

The outline for my termination meetings typically all followed the same format. First, I would greet the employee to make them feel as comfortable as possible given the setting. As stated above, I would then review the facts that led us to our current situation. I would then let the employee know that after reviewing all the facts, the decision had been made to move forward with terminating employment effective immediately. Most of the time there was a document to sign so I would ask that they sign the document showing the separation. At this point, I would let them know the next steps. There are important items that should be covered such as how long benefits will last after termination, returning any company items and getting any personal belongings the employee may have had at their desk. My personal feeling is that you should avoid bringing the employee back out to the work environment, if at all possible, to minimize disruption to the workplace. Once their personal items have been retrieved it is appropriate to walk them out of the building. I always like to end the conversation with a handshake and well-wishes for the future. Just because someone is being terminated from their employment with you, it doesn't make them a bad person. It just means that performance isn't suited for the job or that a mistake was made that is irreparable and a separation is necessary. I've even had employees give me a hug and thank me for making them feel comfortable during the meeting after walking them out of the building. THIS is the reason that I feel strongly that the approach I've outlined works. It has made me more comfortable doing something that I NEVER enjoy doing, and most employees leave the meeting feeling comfortable and with their dignity intact.

Realizing and understanding that performance management is a necessary and an important part of being a leader was a game-changer for me. I was afraid of, and even avoided performance management when I was a new leader when I should have embraced it and utilized it as a tool to achieve greater results. Once I started using the process shown in this chapter it became much easier and eventually the fear went away. Performance started to improve, and I came to the realization that most employees don't hold it against you and aren't that upset if you clearly break down what has occurred in the past and why performance management is necessary. I've even found that by following this approach, in the case that you do have to terminate employment, there are times when the employee will thank you for giving them the opportunities to improve and will apologize for having to let them go. This is about the best scenario you can hope for! By using the process outlined in this chapter, performance management can become easier for you when you are required to do it and drastically improve your organization's results.

Chapter Eleven: Time Management

As a leader you're most likely going to be pulled in many different directions. It is important that you learn the value of time management and set yourself up with a system to help you manage your time most effectively. There isn't necessarily a right way to do this, but there is a wrong way...failing to set up any system at all.

I learned my time management systems through listening and observing top performers to see what they did to efficiently manage their time. I also took a great deal from two books which I'd recommend to anyone. "No Excuses" by Brian Tracy is a phenomenal book with exercises on goal setting and how to achieve a better life. In his book he talks about giving yourself an edge by arriving to the office one hour before anyone else, or before you're scheduled to start. He also recommends working through lunch while still making the time to eat a healthy meal and staying one hour late at the end of your shift. By doing this you're able to accomplish far more because you've gained yourself almost two extra days in the work week. I understand that this may not be possible for those in a non-salaried position, but you can still make this work by utilizing those extra three hours each day to plan your approach to the eight hours that you are on the clock.

The other book which even has a workbook you can go through is "The Perfect Day Formula" by Craig Ballantyne. Craig gets up at 4am every day and while he doesn't say that everyone should do that, his approach is to make sure to attack your most important tasks first thing in the day before things get hectic in the afternoon. He also takes the approach of planning out the day the night before. It gets your mind in the state of knowing what needs to be done the next day and subconsciously getting you ready to wake up early and excited to do what you've prioritized.

At a seminar I attended, the President of the West Division for Comcast Cable, Steve White, shared something similar. He said that every Sunday night he would take some time to plan his next week. Keep in mind that this is when most people are posting memes about how much they hate going to work on Monday. Instead of wasting his time complaining about the work week ahead he was planning what he was going to do to have a successful week! Makes sense that he was one of the top people in a Fortune 50 company!

You may notice that in every example above, it requires putting in extra time. Many people believe that being in a leadership role means they have the freedom to do whatever they want and that they'll be able to work even less. While some people may be able to get away with that for a while, they will eventually be exposed as poor leaders and someone who is willing to do an excellent job will replace them. Every great leader that I've met or worked for put in more time instead of less. If you're reading this and are not yet in a leadership position with your company, be prepared for this reality if you do decide to take that step and move into leadership. It's not for everybody and it's important for those that think they want to be in a leadership position to understand this key fact. I once had a leader say to me that this was their biggest mistake they made as a new leader. They thought they could get everything done and be effective in forty hours. What it got them was to the verge of termination. Once they made the shift to more effectively managing their time and they realized that it was beneficial to put in some extra hours they began to thrive and get great results with their team.

Here I'll share the system that has worked for me and that I've taught to many others to help them with their time management. One of the most important things you can possibly do is to utilize your calendar. I've personally used Outlook, but feel free to use whatever you're comfortable with. I regularly scheduled recurring meetings, coaching sessions and one on ones on my calendar. This way I could plan in advance and make sure that everyone was getting time with me. It amazes me how many people still do not use their calendar. It reminds me of a leaf floating in the wind. They're taken wherever the next crisis is! While you frequently need to adjust plans to handle unexpected things that come up, if you take the step of scheduling your day on the calendar you are not at the whim of whoever may stop by your office. It provides a great structure and I've found it makes your employees more at ease because they know when they will have time scheduled with you.

For my daily routine I would start by making it into the office about an hour before my actual work shift began. During that time, I would list out the previously planned meetings that I had on the calendar, so I had a constant visual reminder of what was needing to be done that day. As I was a sales director in a call center I would look at the previous days call and sales stats to prioritize if there was anyone I needed to prioritize following up with based on the data. From there I had a daily sales and recognition e-mail that I sent to my entire team. I would get that completed before most of my sales professionals had even arrived in the office. During this time, I would also add to my list anything that my boss needed from me that had come up that morning. Once I had everything listed out for the day I would then prioritize most important to least important. At that point I would begin to work on whatever the top priority for the day was. Following the Brian Tracy system of putting in at least an extra hour after the shift ended, I would then look at what I was able to accomplish throughout the day and ensure that all my top priority items had been completed. If there was anything on my list that I couldn't get done, I would assess if it was something that still needed to be done that day. If so I would stay as long as necessary to get it finished. Sometimes there were things that could be completed the following day, so I would make sure they were high on the priority list and on the calendar for the next day. I would take a moment to then preview what I had on the calendar for the next day to ensure I was ready when I came into work the next morning.

Utilizing this system, I was able to stick to a schedule that ensured I was following up with all my employees, while prioritizing certain items that came up throughout the course of the day all while remaining flexible enough to pivot when needed. While I was spending a little more time in the office than many of my peers, I was usually able to get to a level where my teams were performing stronger more quickly because of the extra time I was devoting to my teams and employees. It took stress off me because I had a structure that I followed. It also took stress off the people that reported to me because they knew when they had time scheduled on the calendar with me, while still being aware of my open-door policy.

Time management and the ability to get things done is one of the hallmarks of a good leader. By effectively managing your time you will create less stress for yourself as well as less stress for the employees that report to you. You will find that you're able to accomplish more of the things that are most important and even determine when the best time is to delegate certain tasks. As a leader, be prepared that typically it means you're going to have to work more, not less, but the rewards of effective time management will help you lead high performing, engaged teams.

Chapter Twelve: Meetings & How to Use Them Effectively

For this chapter we'll focus on meetings when there are multiple employees attending with the purpose being an exchange of ideas or information sharing. Coaching and training meetings are a different topic which I'll cover in the next chapter.

There are many different schools of thought when it comes to meetings. Some people love meetings, some people hate meetings and some only like meetings if there's information that's directly relevant to them. Personally, I'm one of those people who have a love/hate relationship with meetings. Meetings are an integral part of doing business. There is value in meeting with someone face to face to talk through an idea, provide training or give an important business update.

Before having a meeting, assess if it's truly necessary and beneficial for those that will be in attendance. I've cancelled many meetings that were on the calendar simply because there wasn't anything relevant to discuss. Oftentimes in those cases, it would be more effective to cover certain items with individuals instead of bringing everybody into the meeting. Once you've determined that you will be having the meeting it is helpful to provide an outline or agenda for what will be covered during the meeting. This helps people stay focused and know where you're at in the meeting. It also helps those who may tend to not enjoy being in meetings to stay engaged because they can see the direction the meeting is going.

If possible, it's also helpful to assign somebody to take notes on what was covered during the meeting. This can be extremely valuable if someone needs to miss the meeting. One other added benefit is that upon reviewing the meeting notes, you can ensure that the content came across the way it was intended to.

I personally have never assigned a timekeeper, but some find it helpful to have someone keep time during the meeting to ensure things stay in the allotted timeframe. It is important to stay on time with your meetings though, so you'll want to put some sort of system in place for yourself to stay on time and on task. Some find it helpful to place a time allocation on the agenda with the topic and presenter so that everyone can stay on pace. For me, it was just having a clock up in the meeting room and making mental notes of what had been covered on the agenda and the time left in the meeting. Whenever possible, try to leave some Q & A time at the end to address any important questions that may arise.

People's attention tends to naturally wane when they're listening to the same person speak for a long period of time. This is the reason why it's important to engage your team and invite participation in the meeting. One common practice to use when it's applicable is to have one of your team members cover the topic on the agenda or lead the discussion. This breaks up the monotony of having one person speak and gives someone else on the team the chance to practice their skills in leading a meeting. Another important thing to remember is to watch the attendees and their level of engagement. It can be very beneficial to ask someone's opinion on a topic that's being discussed. Not only do you get more participation, but you'll probably notice the side effect of having your meeting attendees paying more attention. Few things are more embarrassing than being called on during a meeting and not having anything to say because you weren't paying attention. Everyone has their own strengths and weaknesses. Utilize the members of your team's strengths over the course of the meeting to increase engagement, show they are valued and ultimately get greater results.

Things to Avoid

Earlier in the chapter we touched on not having a meeting just for the sake of having the meeting. This is one of the worst things you can do. You're taking your employees away from their primary duties with no actual reason for doing so. Don't get me wrong, I've seen leaders take their teams outside for a meeting on a nice day with the only topic being to say something they love about working for the company. While it's not exactly my style, I do see value in that. You're improving morale and possibly company loyalty. In this case there's still an intention and reason for the meeting. What I'm talking about is getting everyone together in the meeting room and then not having anything to go over or a game plan. My experience with those kinds of meetings is that it turns into a complaint fest bringing everyone's mood down and decreasing productivity. DO NOT have a meeting just for the sake of having a meeting!

Another item to avoid is allowing things to get out of hand during your meeting. A huge morale killer is to let someone go on and on with negativity. Address the concern, look for a solution and try to get closure on the issue. If you're unable to get closure on the issue let the person know that you'll be happy to meet with them one on one later to address their concerns. Then proceed to the other items on the agenda that need to be covered. I've only had to do this once, but if an attendee is hijacking the meeting with negativity and taking away from the desired outcome of the meeting it can be appropriate to ask them to leave.

Sometimes meetings can get tense. There can be controversial information or policy changes covered that not everyone likes or wants to hear. As the leader of the meeting you'll want to avoid letting your emotions get the best of you. I've been an attendee in meetings where the meeting leader and one of the attendees have gotten into a shouting match. Terrible for morale and not a good look for the leader. If you find that your emotions are running high, take a deep breath, acknowledge that emotions may be getting out of hand and guide the meeting to the next topic. I can't think of one time where it was beneficial to continue a meeting or at least that topic of the meeting after a shouting match has occurred. In that situation, most people just want to be done so they can get out of an uncomfortable situation. This is certainly not the best scenario for exchanging information and having people get something out of it.

Meetings are an important part of business, there's no denying that. With that said, there are right ways and wrong ways to run a meeting and you should never have a meeting just for the sake of having a meeting. Make sure to have an agenda that you plan to follow, have someone take notes if possible and keep your meeting to the allotted time. Review your notes before the meeting to make sure that the information being covered is relevant to the attendees and even feel free to have people who don't really stand to gain anything from the meeting stay back and not attend. Keep the meeting engaging by involving your meeting attendees and even have others take on parts of the meetings at times. Avoid having your meetings hijacked by negativity by first controlling your own emotions and recognizing when things may be starting to get out of hand. By following these guidelines, you will ensure productive and meaningful meetings that your employees will leave having gained useful information.

Chapter Thirteen: Common Mistakes

Wow! There are a lot of mistakes I've made over my career. It's OK to make mistakes as long as you learn from them. I am happy to say that while I am in no way perfect, I have learned greatly from the mistakes I've made over the years. In this chapter I'll lay out some of the mistakes I've made in my career so hopefully you don't have to! Just learn from my mistakes instead. It's much easier that way! Much of what I'll go over in this chapter has been at least touched on at other times in this book. The goal here is to go into more depth on the mistakes that were made and ways to avoid them.

Oversharing

One major mistake I see leaders, both new and tenured, make is sharing too much. While it is good to be transparent and open when you can, there comes a point of diminishing returns. I've seen many leaders want to be the "cool" boss or be known as the one who shares everything with their team. My opinion on this is that you share what will help make your team better or optimize performance.

Here's an example that I personally witnessed and was even questioned by a few members of my team, where information was shared unnecessarily. My boss had shared with the group of managers something that corporate was thinking about doing which would have caused a major shakeup to the call center we were in. At this point it was still uncertain if it was going to happen, how it would affect people or even a timeline. I honestly don't even remember what the change was that was being discussed. What I do remember is that another manager went and told their team about the possibility of the change. Once the word got out to one team, the rumor mill started going and it spread like wildfire throughout the call center. I had one of the supervisors who reported to me come to me and ask about it. I told him that it was something that had been discussed, but that at this point there were no details, nor was there even a timeframe on when the possible change may happen.

The supervisor asked me why I hadn't shared any of the information with my team. I responded with a question. "Was the supervisor who told you about this possible change excited or were they worried?" My team member said that the person they heard the news from was pretty worried. I then asked the question, "do you think hearing that news is helping them lead their team or hurting them?" The supervisor thought about it for a second and responded that it was probably hurting them. Instead of being with their team coaching and working on their improvements they were out talking to other supervisors about something that may or may not happen. I then explained to the supervisor my philosophy on sharing things and it was simple. If what I'm going to share will cause unnecessary stress and anxiety, taking them away from what is important, then I'm not going to share it. In this case, if it was a change that was absolutely going to happen I would share it with them. However, this is something that we weren't even sure was going to be followed through with. I didn't see any point in sharing information that could cause anxiety and stress and the resulting diminished performance. In this particular situation, what was being talked about never even ended up happening. I can see why my boss shared it with us as managers since it was something we should have been aware of as a possibility, but it was unnecessary for me to share it with anyone else until there were more details and certainty that it was going to occur.

About a year later, after that supervisor had moved to another department, he came to my office and told me that he now understood why I didn't always share everything with my team. He said his new boss tended to share everything whether it was going to happen or not and it caused a lot of stress and anxiety for the people on his team. He said that now that he was seeing things from a different perspective he appreciated that I tried to shield them from that additional pressure and allow them to focus on their primary job, which was growing and developing their teams. Share what is necessary and anything that will help your team improve but guard those things that will cause additional stress and anxiety if it's not relevant to your people.

Spending Too Much Time on E-Mail

One of the most common mistakes I see and hear about from new leaders is spending too much time on e-mail. It is very common for a leader to think that they need to be behind their desk and respond to every e-mail that comes through within minutes. The truth is that if something is that urgent, the manager will just come find you or call you on the phone. I can't think of one time in my career that I got into any type of trouble or even created a major hardship for my boss because I didn't respond to an e-mail right away. Even as you're running your team you'll find that if they need something followed up on immediately they will just come ask you.

The trap with being so engaged with e-mail is that some leaders fail to personally engage with their teams. You will always get better results by being out with your employees, coaching and talking with them about what challenges they're facing. If it's an environment where employees are more self-sufficient and working on projects, the simple act of talking with them for a moment and giving them encouragement for the good job they are doing will do more for you than staying behind your desk all day looking at e-mails.

The system I learned after watching and learning from many top performers is to set aside time each day to handle e-mails. One of the best things you can do is to plan out your day using some sort of calendar whether that be through your phone, your company e-mail system or even just writing it out. In any case have a way that works for you to plan, prioritize and track your activities throughout the day. What worked best for me was to get in the office early before my team was in and handle any e-mails that may have come through overnight. This way I could also prioritize anything that did need to be followed up on right away. I would also set about thirty minutes aside during the middle of the day, typically right after lunch, to check any e-mails that had come in that may need more immediate attention. Finally, I would set about an hour aside after my team had left to check any other e-mails and follow up on those that I deemed to be less urgent. This way I was handling e-mails when I didn't have my people there to help and be engaged with. Not everyone is going to be able to put in the extra time, so you may have to schedule it differently than I did, but the point is to schedule it on your calendar and stick to the schedule. This way you won't fall into the trap, as so many do, of spending your entire day on e-mails and not actually getting anything done!

Prioritizing the Wrong Things

One way that new leaders, and even some tenured ones, prioritize ineffectively is determining what needs to be done by you and what can be done by others. I'm not necessarily talking about delegating here, but I'm sure there are places where it applies there as well. I'll illustrate this point with a story about a new leader I had the pleasure of having on my team. Another leader in the organization who had a top performing team had volunteered for a special project that had him hanging some strategic decorations designed to help boost morale and improve overall performance. The new leader was returning from lunch when the tenured leader spotted him and asked if he would be interested in helping with the project. The new leader, being eager to help, enthusiastically said that of course he would. I overheard the interaction and recognized an excellent opportunity for a coaching moment for both supervisors who happened to report to me. I asked the tenured leader where his team was ranked to which he responded that he was in the top five. This was out of about forty teams we had at the time. I then asked the new leader where his team was ranked. He responded that they were last place. I asked the new leader how him helping with a project that would take him away from his team would help them move up the ranks to no longer be a last place team. After thinking for a moment, he admitted that it would not help them at all. I then asked him what the best use of his time would be to move the team in the right direction. He said time would be much better spent coaching the team. I agreed with him and made the point to say that while the tenured leader should be helping with special projects because he had built his team into a top performing team already, it was not the place where a new leader with a poor performing team should be spending his time. This is something that I see very frequently. New leaders are so excited to be in the position and eager to help, that they forget the primary duties and what will truly be the best benefit to the company-leading their teams. Let the supervisors who are tenured and have gotten their teams to a level where they are performing take on the special tasks and projects that are also important to the business. In this way, the business and the employees win! For those reading this book who may be managing supervisors, don't be afraid to question a supervisor's activities and coach when it is necessary. I've also witnessed far too many managers allow supervisors with lower performing teams to spend time doing special projects away from their teams which is ultimately a detriment to the business.

Thinking You Need to Know Everything

So, you've been promoted into a leadership position and now have a team of people that report to you. You need to know everything right away when you're asked, or you won't appear to be as good of a leader right? Wrong! Many leaders think they need to have an answer immediately. Some will even go as far as to make something up, so they don't lose face in front of a team member because they don't know the real answer. Honestly, I think I would have probably fallen into this trap myself early on as a leader, but I stumbled onto something during one of my initial meetings with my team when I became a supervisor. In Chapter One we discussed getting to know your team and building credibility. I was doing just that and asked the question of the team I had taken over what they liked about their previous leader and some of what they didn't like so much. The team told me something that stuck with me to this day. They said "the previous supervisor would just give an answer when we asked a question, even if it was wrong. He didn't want to look like he didn't know so he would just answer with what he thought it was without actually knowing and if we questioned further he would get angry with us." When they said this, it made me think back to how many times I had asked a question of a supervisor and left the conversation not feeling confident in the answer because it appeared that the supervisor had decided to just "wing it" with their answer. I resolved that I would take the approach that if I didn't know the answer to something I would find it and get back to that person as soon as possible. There's no shame in telling someone that you're helping that you don't know the answer, but that you'll find it. The key is you need to find the answer and get back to them or you lose all credibility! People feel much better about an honest answer of "I don't know, but I'll find out for you" than an answer that may be completely off-base. I truly appreciate that first team I ever had, giving me that nugget of wisdom! They saved me from making a very common mistake that new leaders make. This powerful point was illustrated to me via feedback from a team that reported to me. They shared, "we appreciate that if you don't know the answer to something you'll tell us I don't know...and then find the correct answer for us right away!"

Executive Presence

When you become a leader, you're expected to handle yourself a certain way. That can encompass the way you dress, the way you talk, how you carry yourself, etc. We'll start with the easiest one...how you dress or your appearance. I say this is the easiest because it doesn't require that you do anything other than make the choice to put some effort into what kind of impression you make. I learned this one early on, but unfortunately, I didn't always practice it until I was reminded of it later in my career. Toward the beginning of my sales career, I was part of an elite team selling mattresses in a call center. Everyone on this team had been hand chosen or promoted into the position based on their sales results or potential. As a result, the team made the decision that we wanted to "look the part". We bought custom polo shirts that represented the team and regularly wore slacks and ties in a work environment where many came to work in their pajamas! Not only were we an elite team in terms of our sales, but we also were an elite team in the way we presented ourselves. We made the choice that we wanted to look like professionals and it made us stand out. Years later, after being a little inconsistent with how I was presenting myself, I read something in a book by Brian Tracy called "No Excuses". In the book it states, "determine the person who is the best dressed and groomed in your company and then resolve to use him/her as a role model for your own appearance." From that point on I dressed up and wore a tie almost every day to the point where many commented that I was one of, if not the best dressed person where I worked. You know what? It made a difference in how I felt about myself and in how I was perceived by others. Think about it…if you roll out of bed and come into work sloppy and not well groomed as a leader will your team really take you that seriously? If you can't set the example to care about how you come across how are they supposed to care? Some will say that it's not politically correct and people don't make judgements based on appearance anymore. The research studies from Psychology Today to The New York Times show otherwise. Appearance does matter so think about what message you're portraying with how you choose to present yourself on a day to day basis. To further illustrate this point, I had a supervisor who, once he started reporting to me, decided to start dressing up for work. Instead of wanting to always be "comfortable" he shifted his mindset and appearance to always wanting to be "sharp". He even began wearing suits to work in an environment that was more on the casual side of business casual. The result, he shared with me, was that he felt better about himself and noticed that he was also getting more respect from his team. It doesn't take much more effort or even much more money, but by putting a little thought into your appearance and how you present yourself you can make a huge difference in your results and career.

Another piece that goes along with "executive presence" is how you talk. When you're a leader, everything you say holds some weight whether you realize it or not. You have people looking to you for guidance and direction. If you're constantly talking negatively about other people, processes or the company in general it sets the tone for your workgroup. While this one is a little more difficult, I do believe it is also a choice. Make the choice to only speak words that are positive and uplifting. Don't gossip or commiserate at lunch about how bad things are. Be the person that people want to go to for a dose of positivity. I'm not saying to not be realistic...there are times when things aren't going well. However, don't dwell on the negative. Actively look for the positive and how you can be the one that brings positivity to the situation. This will have a huge effect on the morale of your team and even just those who you encounter on a daily basis. They will greatly appreciate you for it! I once received what I felt like was a phenomenal compliment. An employee who I had previously worked with called me because he said he "just wanted a dose of positivity". I was no longer with the company, but the employee told his boss that he was going to give me a call purely because I was positive and motivating. The choice to be a positive leader and to present yourself that way will have a major lasting impact!

Not Asking for Help

In doing research for this book I asked several current leaders what some of the lessons were that they wish they would have learned earlier. A common theme was not asking for help! This one honestly surprised me a little bit, but that's probably because I'm the type who is constantly looking for and asking for feedback. I think this one also ties into the concept of thinking you need to know everything as a leader. Maybe there's the perception that you'll be looked down on by your leader for not knowing something. It's OK to not know everything and you're expected to ask for help, especially when you're a new leader! As a matter of fact, I've called out supervisors who reported to me for not asking enough questions! I personally would rather have someone ask a ton of questions than not ask any. If you're not asking questions, I'm going to think that maybe you don't really care that much about what you're doing. It's perfectly fine to make mistakes, but why make them if you don't have to? Utilize your leader to help guide you as you progress as a leader. Chances are good that they've seen or experienced any challenges you're facing and will have some good insight to help you overcome the obstacles in your way sooner rather than later.

Along these same lines is not sharing your vision or what you want to accomplish with your leader. Again, this was never an issue for me as I was possibly too vocal about what I wanted to do and achieve. However, I would rather be too vocal in this regard than not vocal enough and not get the help and support that I need to accomplish my goals. Make sure to be very clear with your manager about what you want to achieve and then follow their advice to help you get there faster.

As I previously mentioned, these two things were never problems for me. I believe the reason for that is that I was very proactive in knowing what I wanted, knowing that I would need help getting there, and being very open to any advice or feedback that could help me get there. Here's what worked for me...

Not every manager is going to be a "hands-on" leader. In fact, many that I've worked with would rather step back and let the employee do their work only intervening when the employee asks for help or if something is going wrong. Many employees enjoy this approach because they don't feel like they're being micro-managed. If you have a manager like this, but you're the type who wants to have a manager who is more involved, you're going to need to be proactive in the relationship.

The first step is to specifically ask for regular time on the calendar. Set up a meeting cadence that works for both of you. The next step is to come to each meeting prepared. This is especially important if you do have a manager that doesn't like to regularly meet. They might initially see the meeting as a waste of time, so you want to make sure and have specific things that you want to cover during the meeting. I usually wrote down the top three to five things I was working on or needed help with at that moment. This would help guide the conversation and keep things moving in the right direction so that I got the most out of the time spent together. Take notes during the meeting so you can reference them later. This will not only help you to remember what was discussed, but it will also show your manager that you are taking an active role in the meeting to fully get something out of your time spent together. Finally, practice and use what you learned or got out of the meeting! I personally liked to report back to my manager what the result was when I had used something they shared with me. There were two reasons...and both were admittedly pretty selfish now that I think about it! One was that it showed my manager that I was truly getting something from our meetings together and was using what they taught me. My thought was that by me showing my manager what I was gaining from our meetings, they would see the value and ensure that we continued meeting. The second was that by sharing what I had learned, it reinforced the message in my brain and helped to cement the lesson in my subconscious.

Allowing an Employee to Dominate Your Team

This happens more often in performance driven environments such as sales, but it will end up being detrimental to your team and organization in any environment. What happens is that someone on the team will be so successful that they start doing whatever they want. This may mean they show up to work late, don't make or take the number of calls required by the business or even in some extreme cases are unprofessional in the workplace. The trap some leaders fall into is that because the employee is such a strong performer they are allowed to write their own rules. The leader that lets this happen is making a huge mistake!

You may even think you're doing right by the business by allowing them to continue with their behavior if they are performing or "writing numbers". I'm not even going to approach this subject from an HR perspective as this chapter could go on and on about the risks associated with working this way. Instead, I'll approach it from the perspective of how it damages you as the leader and the organization overall.

I had a conversation with a supervisor who was struggling with an employee that had been with the company since the beginning. This employee was allowed to have a different schedule than the rest of the office, allowed to behave unprofessionally during team meetings with minimal consequences, did not make the expected number of calls each day and did not follow the dress code that the rest of the office had to adhere to. The supervisor was frustrated because the founders of the company were the ones allowing this to happen. When the supervisor brought up the fact that the employee was playing by a different set of rules than everyone else, he was told to just leave the employee alone since they hit their sales goals every month.

Some still may not see any problem with this situation. Here are the issues you open yourself up to as the leader if you allow this to occur...

Respect-the rest of the team sees that someone is not playing by the rules and wonders why the leader of the team allows it to continue. Eventually, they will lose respect for the leader because it's clear that the leader is not controlling the team or the working environment.

Disorder-as employees see that the culture rewards those who hit numbers and that those who are "performing" can pretty much do as they please, more and more people will try to push the envelope. This will result in chaos within your organization. It is very difficult to reign things back in once they've gotten to this point. It is much easier and more effective to start tight and loosen up than it is to start relaxed and then tighten things up in the business later. You risk killing employee morale by either not addressing the employee or trying to right the ship later after things have fallen into disarray.

Loss of Control-I once worked with a supervisor, James Buck III who used to say, "don't let the inmates run the asylum". I've witnessed times where a supervisor put so much trust and faith in their top employee that eventually the team stopped listening to the supervisor and would only listen to the top performer on the team. What started as good intentions by the supervisor to give a top employee more responsibility and prepare them for leadership backfired when the employee started to vocally disagree with the leader during team meetings. Naturally, with so much faith put into the employee by the rest of the team, it caused a very negative reaction by many on the team and backlash to the supervisor. It took a lot of work for that supervisor to regain control of the team.

Negativity-this ties into everything else we've already discussed, but I feel it is important to still give it its own bullet point. Often when an employee gets to the point where they are dominating the team, they are not a positive and uplifting influence. You'll find them talking bad about the company, the leaders, the policies and any changes that are happening in the business. This negativity spreads like wildfire and because the supervisor has put too much faith in the employee or allowed them to dominate the team, many other employees will jump on the negativity bandwagon.

Allowing an employee to dominate your team or get special treatment can essentially sabotage your team or organization. You'll see how detrimental it can be and the trickle-down effect it has on everybody in the organization. A quote from coach and leadership expert John Wooden that I love and think applies here is "the star of the team is the team."

I truly do believe that leaders are made and not born. In your journey through leadership you're going to make many mistakes. This is perfectly fine and is to be expected! The most important part is that you learn from the mistakes that you make. The goal of this chapter, and really this book in general, is to give you the tools to be able to avoid the major mistakes that many leaders make. It takes hard work, resilience, an open mind and a desire to learn and grow no matter the challenges you are faced with. By taking this approach you will find that the journey becomes easier and you will have the support that you need to evolve into an effective leader that helps grow people and the organization!

Chapter Fourteen: Continuing Education and Growing Your Skills

A 2018 study by Pew Research stated that 24% of American adults say they haven't read a book in whole or in part in the past year, whether in print, electronic or audio form. A 2015 study by CNN Money showed a surprising statistic...Americans spent almost five times more money on lottery tickets, $70.1 billion, than they did on books, $14.6 billion! Contrast that with the often-cited survey that states the average CEO reads around five books each month! While I won't get into any political or moral commentary, I think it's clear what people value. You're already setting yourself apart from the masses by making it this far in this book!

One of the best things you can do as a leader, not just for yourself but also for your team, is to resolve to continue to learn and expand your skills. It will expose you to new ideas, different ways of thinking and may even change your life. Reading is just one of the ways to do this. There are also audio and video programs, seminars and even YouTube videos that can help you grow as a leader.

As a young sales professional I picked up a copy of Dale Carnegie's How to Win Friends and Influence People. It was critical in my development not only in my work in sales, but also in how I communicated with people in general. I found myself able to connect with a greater variety of people and hold more meaningful conversations utilizing the skills and techniques I learned from reading that book.

In 2014 I picked up a copy of Brian Tracy's "No Excuses". Reading that book helped me improve in the areas of self-discipline and goal setting. I now read this book once a year and have found that since applying the principles I've learned through this book I have been able to increase my income year over year nearly doubling where I was at prior to reading the book!

In 2016 I was introduced to the Jason Capital YouTube channel through a friend of mine. At the time Jason Capital was transitioning from a dating coach to an income and success coach. I watched all the videos I could find and invested in some of the programs that Jason had on his website. I even attended his seminar in Newport Beach, California where I was exposed to even more great speakers and coaches! Through following the free content on YouTube, the content I purchased through the website and the exposure I received at the live event I made the choice to follow my dream of living somewhere with a nicer climate than the Pacific Northwest where I grew up. I made the move to the Phoenix; Arizona area and it has been one of the best decisions I've ever made even though it was a great risk.

I share these things to illustrate how continuing education has made a big impact in my life with the hope that it may do the same for you. I truly believe that the decision to continue to educate yourself and grow your skills has the potential to be life altering for you and for those around you. Nobody forced me to read those books or watch those videos. Nobody forced you to pick up this book today! It's a decision that we made to better ourselves and improve our skills. As a leader, you're not only leading your team. You're leading by example in everything you do and therefore affecting all those that you encounter. Making the choice to better yourself will be seen by others and will have a lasting impact. Share what you've learned with those around you so that you can uplift them as well. Had my friend not shared with me what he was learning, I may have never made the move to Arizona or wrote this book! I am forever grateful to have friends that were growing themselves and then shared that growth with me and I know your friends and family will appreciate it too!

Since you made it this far in this book I'm guessing you're already the type of person that is constantly looking to learn, grow, and upgrade your skills. If you haven't been that way in the past, resolve today to make life-long learning a part of your DNA. Not only will you continue to grow as a person and add more value to those around you, but you will also find that it helps to grow your personal income!

I applaud you for taking a great step in becoming a better leader and for equipping yourself with additional tools to help you in your leadership journey. If you're an aspiring leader, the simple fact that you picked up and read this book will help you greatly in your professional development and help you to avoid many of the mistakes that I and many other leaders made early on in our leadership careers. I hope you've found the examples and experiences shared in this book to be helpful and entertaining. Use this as a handbook and refer to the situations shared in this book to help yourself when faced with the challenges that come up when you're a leader. Please share any success stories you experience that are a result of applying the principles from this book at www.shiningbeaconleadership.com. I hope for an abundance of success for you in both your personal and professional life!